MERCURY READER

a custom publication

Professor R. Edmunds
English 1A
Yuba College

Pearson Learning Solutions

New York   Boston   San Francisco
London   Toronto   Sydney   Tokyo   Singapore   Madrid
Mexico City   Munich   Paris   Cape Town   Hong Kong   Montreal

Senior Vice President, Editorial and Marketing: Patrick F. Boles
Senior Sponsoring Editor: Natalie Danner
Development Editor: Mary Kate Paris
Editorial Assistant: Jill Johnson
Marketing Manager: Brian T. Berkeley
Operations Manager: Eric M. Kenney
Production Manager: Jennifer Berry
Rights Manager: Jillian Santos
Art Director: Renée Sartell
Cover Designers: Kristen Kiley, Blithe Russo, Tess Mattern, and Renée Sartell

Cover Art: "Gigantia Mountains & Sea of Cortes," by R.G.K. Photography, Copyright © Tony Stone Images; "Dime," courtesy of the Shaw Collection; "Open Book On Table Edge w/Pencil," courtesy of PhotoAlto Photography/Veer Incorporated; "Open Book On Table Near Table's Corner," courtesy of Fancy Photography/Veer Incorporated; "Scrabble Pieces and a Die," by G. Herbst, courtesy of PlainPicture Photography/Veer Incorporated; "Binary codes in bowls," by John Still, courtesy of Photographer's Choice/Getty Images; "Close-up of an open book," courtesy of Glowimages/Getty Images; "College Students Sitting At Tables," courtesy of Blend/PunchStock; "Red and blue circles," courtesy of Corbis Images; "Laptop screen showing photograph of landscape," courtesy of Martin Holtcamp/Getty Images; "Apples flying," courtesy of Arne Morgenstern/Getty Images.

Please visit our website at *www.pearsoncustom.com.*

Attention bookstores: For permission to return any unsold stock, contact us at *pe-uscustomreturns@pearson.com.*

Pearson Learning Solutions, 501 Boylston Street, Suite 900, Boston, MA 02116
A Pearson Education Company
www.pearsoned.com

1 2 3 4 5 6 7 8 9 10 V202 14 13 12 11 10 09

ISBN 10: 0-558-17882-0
ISBN 13: 978-0-558-17882-6

Contents

Education

Don't You Think It's Time to Start Thinking?

Northrop Frye

Northrop Frye (1912–1991), one of Canada's most distinguished scholars, was reared in New Brunswick, and after attending school in Canada, received his MA from Oxford University, in England (1940). In 1939 Frye became a professor at the University of Toronto, where he wrote and taught until his death. His interests were literary criticism and school curriculum; his books include On Education *and* Myth and Metaphor. *The following essay insists that thinking happens only when a person writes down ideas "in the right words."*

1 A student often leaves high school today without any sense of language as a structure.

He may also have the idea that reading and writing are elementary skills that he mastered in childhood, never having grasped the fact that there are differences in levels of reading and writing as there are in mathematics between short division and integral calculus.

Yet, in spite of his limited verbal skills, he firmly believes that he can think, that he has ideas, and that if he is just given the opportunity to express them he will be all right. Of course, when you look at what he's written you find it doesn't make any sense. When you tell him this he is devastated.

Part of his confusion here stems from the fact that we use the word "think" in so many bad, punning ways. Remember James Thurber's Walter Mitty who was always dreaming great dreams of glory. When his wife asked him what he was doing he would say, "Has it ever occurred to you that I might be thinking?"

But, of course, he wasn't thinking at all. Because we use it for every- thing our minds do, worrying, remembering, daydreaming, we imag- ine that thinking is something that can be achieved without any training. But again it's a matter of practice. How well we can think depends on how much of it we have already done. Most students need to be taught, very carefully and patiently, that there is no such thing as an inarticu- late idea waiting to have the right words wrapped around it.

They have to learn that ideas do not exist until they have been incorporated into words. Until that point you don't know whether you are pregnant or just have gas on the stomach.

The operation of thinking is the practice of articulating ideas until they are in the right words. And we can't think at random either. We can only add one more idea to the body of something we have already thought about. Most of us spend very little time doing this, and that is why there are so few people whom we regard as having any power to articulate at all. When such a person appears in pub- lic life, like Mr. Trudeau, we tend to regard him as possessing a gigan- tic intellect.

A society like ours doesn't have very much interest in literacy. It is compulsory to read and write because society must have docile and obedient citizens. We are taught to read so that we can obey the traffic signs and to cipher so that we can make out our income tax, but development of verbal competency is very much left to the individual.

And when we look at our day-to-day existence we can see that there are strong currents at work against the development of powers of artic- ulateness. Young adolescents today often betray a curious sense of shame about speaking articulately, of framing a sentence with a period at the end of it.

Part of the reason for this is the powerful anti-intellectual drive which is constantly present in our society. Articulate speech marks you out as an individual, and in some settings this can be rather danger- ous because people are often suspicious and frightened of articulate- ness. So if you say as little as possible and use only stereotyped, ready-made phrases you can hide yourself in the mass.

Then there are various epidemics sweeping over society which use unintelligibility as a weapon to preserve the present power struc- ture. By making things as unintelligible as possible, to as many peo- ple as possible, you can hold the present power structure together.

Understanding and articulateness lead to its destruction. This is the kind of thing that George Orwell was talking about, not just in *Nineteen Eighty-Four,* but in all his work on language. The kernel of everything reactionary and tyrannical in society is the impoverishment of the means of verbal communication.

The vast majority of things that we hear today are prejudices and clichés, simply verbal formulas that have no thought behind them but are put up as pretence of thinking. It is not until we realize these things conceal meaning, rather than reveal it, that we can begin to develop our own powers of articulateness.

The teaching of humanities is, therefore, a militant job. Teachers are faced not simply with a mass of misconceptions and unexamined assumptions. They must engage in a fight to help the student confront and reject the verbal formulas and stock responses, to convert passive acceptance into active, constructive power. It is a fight against illiteracy and for the maturation of the mental process, for the development of skills which once acquired will never become obsolete.

Questions on Meaning

1. Frye says that our minds can do many things besides thinking—worrying, remembering, and daydreaming, for example. Why does he say that these are not thinking?
2. What is the difference between reading to understand a traffic sign and reading to understand a play such as *Romeo and Juliet*? Why does Frye think that the distinction is so important?
3. Are the vast majority of things people say prejudices and cliches? Frye says that they are and that people in power want it that way. Why does he think that this is true? Why does he refer to the novel *1984*?

Questions on Style and Structure

1. The style of this essay is sometimes quite forceful, such as "you don't know whether you are pregnant or just have gas." Why does this kind of style make Frye's point? What do we know about his feelings on the subject?
2. In this essay, Frye argues that humanities teachers are important, but he gets to his point at the end of the essay. What effect does this structure have on the reader?
3. Frye uses a forceful style in this essay because he feels strongly about his subject and he wants teachers to see how important their job really is. Find words and phrases that show the power of his emotions, and explain those emotions.

Writing Assignments

1. Find out about George Orwell. What political and social conditions caused Orwell to write his pessimistic novel *1984*? Write about the dangers of controlling people's thoughts.
2. Interview one of your humanities (history, literature, political science, philosophy) teachers. Ask the teacher about the responsibilities of the humanities to human freedom. Write about the interview, using your own responses as well as the teacher's perspectives.
3. Frye wrote in the second half of the twentieth century. Write about examples of complacency or laziness in political or social thought in the twenty-first century. How much have things changed? How much have they remained the same?

Future Shlock

Neil Postman

Neil Postman (1931–2003) was born in Brooklyn, New York. He was educated at the State University of New York and Columbia, and he taught communications arts and sciences at New York University. A well-known spokesman for educational reform, Postman wrote for a number of periodicals, including the Atlantic *and* The Nation. *Publications include* Teaching as a Conserving Activity *(1980),* The Disappearance of Childhood *(1982),* Amusing Ourselves to Death: Public Discourse in the Age of Show Business *(1985), and* Conscientious Objections: Stirring Up Trouble About Language, Technology, and Education *(1988). Also, he coauthored* Linguistics: A Revolution in Teaching *(1966),* Teaching as a Subversive Activity *(1969), and* The Soft Revolution *(1971). Postman edited* Et Cetera, *the journal of general semantics, for a decade. In this essay, Postman attacked the trivialization of American culture and the loss of intelligent discourse by the show business mindset of mass media.*

1 Human intelligence is among the most fragile things in nature. It doesn't take much to distract it, suppress it, or even annihilate it. In this century, we have had some lethal examples of how easily and quickly intelligence can be defeated by any one of its several nemeses: ignorance, superstition, moral fervor, cruelty, cowardice, neglect. In the late 1920s, for example, Germany was, by any measure, the most literate, cultured nation in the world. Its legendary seats of learning attracted scholars from every corner. Its philosophers, social critics, and scientists were of the first rank; its humane traditions an inspiration to less favored nations. But by the mid-1930s—that

is, in less than ten years—this cathedral of human reason had been transformed into a cesspool of barbaric irrationality. Many of the most intelligent products of German culture were forced to flee—for example, Einstein, Freud, Karl Jaspers, Thomas Mann, and Stefan Zweig. Even worse, those who remained were either forced to submit their minds to the sovereignty of primitive superstition, or—worse still—willingly did so: Konrad Lorenz, Werner Heisenberg, Martin Heidegger, Gerhardt Hauptmann. On May 10, 1933, a huge bonfire was kindled in Berlin and the books of Marcel Proust, André Gide, Emile Zola, Jack London, Upton Sinclair, and a hundred others were committed to the flames, amid shouts of idiot delight. By 1936, Joseph Paul Goebbels, Germany's Minister of Propaganda, was issuing a proclamation which began with the following words: "Because this year has not brought an improvement in art criticism, I forbid once and for all the continuance of art criticism in its past form, effective as of today." By 1936, there was no one left in Germany who had the brains or courage to object.

Exactly why the Germans banished intelligence is a vast and largely unanswered question. I have never been persuaded that the desperate economic depression that afflicted Germany in the 1920s adequately explains what happened. To quote Aristotle: Men do not become tyrants in order to keep warm. Neither do they become stupid—at least not *that* stupid. But the matter need not trouble us here. I offer the German case only as the most striking example of the fragility of human intelligence. My focus here is the United States in our own time, and I wish to worry you about the rapid erosion of our own intelligence. If you are confident that such a thing cannot happen, your confidence is misplaced, I believe, but it is understandable.

After all, the United States is one of the few countries in the world founded by intellectuals—men of wide learning, of extraordinary rhetorical powers, of deep faith in reason. And although we have had our moods of anti-intellectualism, few people have been more generous in support of intelligence and learning than Americans. It was the United States that initiated the experiment in mass education that is, even today, the envy of the world. It was America's churches that laid the foundation of our admirable system of higher education; it was the Land-Grant Act of 1862 that made possible our great state universities; and it is to America that scholars and writers have fled when freedom of the intellect became impossible in their own nations. This is why the great historian of American civilization Henry Steele Commager called

America "the Empire of Reason." But Commager was referring to the United States of the eighteenth and nineteenth centuries. What term he would use for America today, I cannot say. Yet he has observed, as others have, a change, a precipitous decline in our valuation of intelligence, in our uses of language, in the disciplines of logic and reason, in our capacity to attend to complexity. Perhaps he would agree with me that the Empire of Reason is, in fact, gone, and that the most apt term for America today is the Empire of Shlock.

In any case, this is what I wish to call to your notice: the frightening displacement of serious, intelligent public discourse in American culture by the imagery and triviality of what may be called show business. I do not see the decline of intelligent discourse in America leading to the barbarisms that flourished in Germany, of course. No scholars, I believe, will ever need to flee America. There will be no bonfires to burn books. And I cannot imagine any proclamations forbidding once and for all art criticism, or any other kind of criticism. But this is not a cause for complacency, let alone celebration. A culture does not have to force scholars to flee to render them impotent. A culture does not have to burn books to assure that they will not be read. And a culture does not need a Minister of Propaganda issuing proclamations to silence criticism. There are other ways to achieve stupidity, and it appears that, as in so many other things, there is a distinctly America way.

5   To explain what I am getting at, I find it helpful to refer to two 5 films, which taken together embody the main lines of my argument. The first film is of recent vintage and is called *The Gods Must Be Crazy*. It is about a tribal people who live in the Kalahari Desert plains of southern Africa, and what happens to their culture when it is invaded by an empty Coca-Cola bottle tossed from the window of a small plane passing overhead. The bottle lands in the middle of the village and is construed by these gentle people to be a gift from the gods, for they not only have never seen a bottle before but have never seen glass either. The people are almost immediately charmed by the gift, and not only because of its novelty. The bottle, it turns out, has multiple uses, chief among them the intriguing music it makes when one blows into it.

But gradually a change takes place in the tribe. The bottle becomes an irresistible preoccupation. Looking at it, holding it, thinking of things to do with it displace other activities once thought essential. But more than this, the Coke bottle is the only thing these people have ever seen of which there is only one of its kind. And so those who do not have it try to get it from the one who does. And the one who does refuses to give it up. Jealousy, greed, and even violence enter the scene, and come very close to destroying the harmony that has characterized their culture for a thousand years. The people begin to love their bottle more than they love themselves, and are saved only when the leader of the tribe, convinced that the gods must be crazy, returns the bottle to the gods by throwing it off the top of a mountain.

The film is great fun and it is also wise, mainly because it is about a subject as relevant to people in Chicago or Los Angeles or New York as it is to those of the Kalahari Desert. It raises two questions of extreme importance to our situation: How does a culture change when new technologies are introduced to it? And is it always desirable for a culture to accommodate itself to the demands of new technologies? The leader of the Kalahari tribe is forced to confront these questions in a way that Americans have refused to do. And because his vision is not obstructed by a belief in what Americans call "technological progress," he is able with minimal discomfort to decide that the songs of the Coke bottle are not so alluring that they are worth admitting envy, egotism, and greed to a serene culture.

The second film relevant to my argument was made in 1967. It is Mel Brooks's first film, *The Producers*. *The Producers* is a rather raucous comedy that has at its center a painful joke: An unscrupulous theatrical producer has figured out that it is relatively easy to turn a buck by producing a play that fails. All one has to do is induce dozens of backers to invest in the play by promising them exorbitant percentages of its profits. When the play fails, there being no profits to disperse, the producer walks away with thousands of dollars that can never be claimed. Of course, the central problem he must solve is to make sure that his play is a disastrous failure. And so he hits upon an excellent idea: he will take the most tragic and grotesque story of our century—the rise of Adolf Hitler—and make it into a musical.

Because the producer is only a crook and not a fool, he assumes that the stupidity of making a musical on this theme will be immediately grasped by audiences and that they will leave the theater in dumbfounded rage. So he calls his play *Springtime for Hitler*, which is also the name of its most important song. The song begins with the words:

Springtime for Hitler and Germany;
Winter for Poland and France.

The melody is catchy, and when the song is sung it is accompa-
nied by a happy chorus line. (One must understand, of course, that
Springtime for Hitler is no spoof of Hitler, as was, for example, Charlie
Chaplin's *The Great Dictator*. The play is instead a kind of denial of
Hitler in song and dance; as if to say, it was all in fun.)

The ending of the movie is predictable. The audience loves the play
and leaves the theater humming *Springtime for Hitler*. The musical
becomes a great hit. The producer ends up in jail, his joke having turned
back on him. But Brooks's point is that the joke is on us. Although the
film was made years before a movie actor became President of the
United States, Brooks was making a kind of prophecy about that—
namely, that the producers of American culture will increasingly turn
our history, politics, religion, commerce, and education into forms of
entertainment, and that we will become as a result a trivial people, incapable of coping with complexity, ambiguity, uncertainty, perhaps even
reality. We will become, in a phrase, a people amused into stupidity.

For those readers who are not inclined to take Mel Brooks as seriously as I do, let me remind you that the prophecy I attribute here to
Brooks was, in fact, made many years before by a more formidable
social critic than he. I refer to Aldous Huxley, who wrote *Brave New
World* at the time that the modern monuments to intellectual stupidity
were taking shape: Nazism in Germany, fascism in Italy, communism in
Russia. But Huxley was not concerned in his book with such naked and
crude forms of intellectual suicide. He saw beyond them, and mostly,
I must add, he saw America. To be more specific he foresaw that the
greatest threat to the intelligence and humane creativity of our culture
would not come from Big Brother and Ministries of Propaganda, or
gulags and concentration camps. He prophesied, if I may put it this
way, that there is tyranny lurking lurking in a Coca-Cola bottle; that we
could be ruined not by what we fear and hate but by what we welcome
and love, by what we construe to be a gift from the gods.

And in case anyone missed his point in 1932, Huxley wrote *Brave
New World Revisited* twenty years later. By then, George Orwell's *1984*
has been published, and it was inevitable that Huxley would compare
Orwell's book with his own. The difference, he said, is that in Orwell's
book people are controlled by inflicting pain. In *Brave New World,*
they are controlled by inflicting pleasure.

The Coke bottle that has fallen in our midst is a corporation of
dazzling technologies whose forms turn all serious public business into

Thesis

a kind of *Springtime for Hitler* musical. Television is the principal instrument of this disaster, in part because it is the medium Americans most dearly love, and in part because it has become the command center of our culture. Americans turn to television not only for their light entertainment but for their news, their weather, their politics, their religion, their history—all of which may be said to be their serious entertainment. The light entertainment is not the problem. The least dangerous things on television are its junk. What I am talking about is television's preemption of our culture's most serious business. It would be merely banal to say that television presents us with entertaining subject matter. It is quite another thing to say that on television all subject matter is presented as entertaining. And that is how television brings ruin to any intelligent understanding of public affairs.

15   Political campaigns, for example, are now conducted largely in   15
the form of television commercials. Candidates forgo precision, complexity, substance—in some cases, language itself—for the arts of show business: music, imagery, celebrities, theatrics. Indeed, political figures have become so good at this, and so accustomed to it, that they do television commercials even when they are not campaigning, as, for example, Geraldine Ferraro for Diet Pepsi and former vice-presidential candidate William Miller and the late Senator Sam Ervin for American Express. Even worse, political figures appear on variety shows, soap operas, and sitcoms. George McGovern, Ralph Nader, Ed Koch, and Jesse Jackson have all hosted "Saturday Night Live." Henry Kissinger and former President Gerald Ford have done cameo roles on "Dynasty." Tip O'Neill and Governor Michael Dukakis have appeared on "Cheers." Richard Nixon did a short stint on "Laugh-In." The late Senator from Illinois, Everett Dirksen, was on "What's My Line?" a prophetic question if ever there was one. What *is* the line of these people? Or, more precisely, *where* is the line that one ought to be able to draw between politics and entertainment? I would suggest that television has annihilated it.

It is significant, I think, that although our current President, a former Hollywood movie actor, rarely speaks accurately and never precisely, he is known as the Great Communicator; his telegenic charm appears to be his major asset, and that seems to be quite good enough in an entertainment-oriented politics. But lest you think his election to two terms is a mere aberration, I must remind you that, as I write [1988], Charlton Heston is being mentioned as a possible candidate for the

10

Republican nomination in 1988. Should this happen, what alternative would the Democrats have but to nominate Gregory Peck? Two
idols of the silver screen going one on one. Could even the fertile
imagination of Mel Brooks have foreseen this? Heston giving us inti-
mations of Moses as he accepts the nomination; Peck re-creating the
courage of his biblical David as he accepts the challenge of running
against a modern Goliath. Heston going on the stump as Michelan-
gelo; Peck countering with Doughas MacArthur. Heston accusing
Peck of insanity because of *The Boys From Brazil.* Peck replying with
the charge that Heston blew the world up in *Return to Planet of the
Apes. Springtime for Hitler* could be closer than you think.

But politics is only one arena in which serious language has been
displaced by the arts of show business. We have all seen how religion
is packaged on television, as a kind of Las Vegas stage show, devoid of
ritual, sacrality, and tradition. Today's electronic preachers are in no
way like America's evangelicals of the past. Men like Jonathan
Edwards, Charles Finney, and George Whitefield were preachers of
theological depth, authentic learning, and great expository power.
Electronic preachers such as Jimmy Swaggart, Jim Bakker, and Jerry
Falwell are merely performers who exploit television's visual power
and their own charisma for the greater glory of themselves.

We have also seen "Sesame Street" and other educational shows in
which the demands of entertainment take precedence over the rigors
of learning. And we well know how American businessmen, working
under the assumption that potential customers require amusement
rather than facts, use music, dance, comedy, cartoons, and celebrities
to sell their products.

Even our daily news, which for most Americans means television
news, is packaged as a kind of show, featuring handsome news readers, exciting music, and dynamic film footage. Most especially, film
footage. When there is no film footage, there is no story. Stranger still,
commercials may appear anywhere in a news story—before, after, or
in the middle. This reduces all events to trivialities, sources of public
entertainment and little more. After all, how serious can a bombing
in Lebanon be if it is shown to us prefaced by a happy United Airlines
commercial and summarized by a Calvin Klein jeans commercial?
Indeed, television newscasters have added to our grammar a new part
of speech—what may be called the "Now . . . this" conjunction, a
conjunction that does not connect two things, but disconnects them.

When newscasters say, "Now . . . this," they mean to indicate that what you have just heard or seen has no relevance to what you are about to hear or see. There is no murder so brutal, no political blunder so costly, no bombing so devastating that it cannot be erased from our minds by a newscaster saying, "Now . . . this." He means that you have thought long enough on the matter (let us say, for forty seconds) and you must now give your attention to a commercial. Such a situation is not "the news." It is merely a daily version of *Springtime for Hitler*, and in my opinion accounts for the fact that Americans are among the most ill-informed people in the world. To be sure, we know *of* many things; but we know *about* very little.

20   To provide some verification of this, I conducted a survey a few   20
years back on the subject of the Iranian hostage crisis. I chose this subject because it was alluded to on television *every day for more than a year.* I did not ask my subjects for their opinions about the hostage situation. I am not interested in opinion polls; I am interested in knowledge polls. The questions I asked were simple and did not require deep knowledge. For example, Where is Iran? What language do the Iranians speak? Where did the Shah come from? What religion do the Iranians practice, and what are its basic tenets? What does "Ayatollah" mean? I found that almost everybody knew practically nothing about Iran. And those who did know something said they had learned it from *Newsweek* or *Time* or the *New York Times*. Television, in other words, is not the great information machine. It is the great disinformation machine. A most nerve-wracking confirmation of this came some time ago during an interview with the producer and the writer of the TV mini-series *Peter the Great*. Defending the historical inaccuracies in the drama—which included a fabricated meeting between Peter and Sir Isaac Newton—the producer said that no one would watch a dry, historically faithful biography. The writer added that it is better for audiences to learn something that is untrue, if it is entertaining, than not to learn anything at all. And just to put some icing on the cake, the actor who played Peter, Maximilian Schell, remarked that he does not believe in historical truth and therefore sees no reason to pursue it.

I do not mean to say that the trivialization of American public discourse is all accomplished on television. Rather, television is the paradigm for all our attempts at public communication. It conditions our minds to apprehend the world through fragmented pictures and forces other media to orient themselves in that direction. You know the standard question we put to people who have difficulty understanding even simple language: we ask them impatiently, "Do I have to draw a picture for you?" Well, it appears that, like it or not, our culture will draw pictures for us, will explain the world to us in pictures. As a medium for conducting public business, language has receded in importance; it has been moved to the periphery of culture and has been replaced at the center by the entertaining visual image.

Please understand that I am making no criticism of the visual arts in general. That criticism is made by God, not by me. You will remember that in His Second Commandment, God explicitly states that "Thou shalt not make unto thee any graven image, nor any likeness of anything that is in Heaven above, or that is in the earth beneath, or the waters beneath the earth." I have always felt that God was taking a rather extreme postion on this, as is His way. As for myself, I am arguing from the standpoint of a symbolic relativist. Forms of communication are neither good nor bad in themselves. They become good or bad depending on their relationship to other symbols and on the functions they are made to serve within a social order. When a culture becomes overloaded with pictures; when logic and rhetoric lose their binding authority; when historical truth becomes irrelevant; when the spoken or written word is distrusted or makes demands on our attention that we are incapable of giving; when our politics, history, education, religion, public information, and commerce are expressed largely in visual imagery rather than words, then a culture is in serious jeopardy.

Neither do I make a complaint against entertainment. As an old song has it, life is not a highway strewn with flowers. The sight of a few blossoms here and there may make our journey a trifle more endurable. But in America, the least amusing people are our professional entertainers. In our present situation, our preachers, entrepreneurs, politicians, teachers, and journalists are committed to entertaining us through media that do not lend themselves to serious, complex discourse. But these producers of our culture are not to be blamed. They, like the rest of us, believe in the supremacy of technological progress. It has never occurred to us that the gods might be crazy. And even if it did, there is no mountaintop from which we can return what is dangerous to us.

We would do well to keep in mind that there are two ways in which the spirit of a culture may be degraded. In the first—the Orwellian—culture becomes a prison. This was the way of the Nazis, and it appears to be the way of the Russians. In the Second—the Huxleyan—culture becomes a burlesque. This appears to be the way of the Americans. What Huxley teaches is that in the Age of Advanced Technology, spiritual devastation is more likely to come from an enemy with a smiling countenance than from one whose face exudes suspicion and hate. In the Huxleyan prophecy, Big Brother does not watch us, by his choice; we watch him, by ours. When a culture becomes distracted by trivia; when political and social life are redefined as a perpetual round of entertainments; when public conversation becomes a from of baby talk; when a people become, in short, an audience and their public business a vaudeville act, then—Huxley argued—a nation finds itself at risk and culture-death is a clear possibility. I agree.

Questions on Meaning

1. Why does Postman believe that human intelligence is so fragile? What can damage or destroy it? What example does he provide to show the quick destruction of an intelligent society?
2. Explain why the two films Postman describes—*The Gods Must Be Crazy* and *The Producers*— "embody" his argument. What did the tribal leader in the first film do that Postman states Americans have refused to do? What was the "prophecy" of the second film that will, in Postman's words, turn Americans into "a people amused into stupidity"?
3. Why does Postman single out television as the root of the problem?

Questions on Rhetorical Strategy and Style

1. What is the primary rhetorical strategy of this essay? Show where Postman supports it with example, narration, and cause and effect.
2. How does Postman compare and contrast Huxley's *Brave New World* and Orwell's *1984*? What is the major difference between Huxley's future society and the society described by Orwell? During the 20th century, what has been the fate of well-known Orwellian societies, such as Nazi Germany and communist Russia? Why does Postman characterize American society as becoming Huxleyan?
3. How does Postman compare and contrast the cultures of pre-World War II Germany with the United States? Why does he state that scholars will not have to flee America and books will not need to be burned for the American culture to become "stupid"?

Writing Assignments

1. Postman criticizes the presentation and format of television news—show business—as trivializing what should be serious, blurring the lines between what is important (a bombing in Lebanon) to what isn't (Calvin Klein jeans). Study the evening news for a few nights. Determine how much time is spent on serious news, human interest, and advertising. Note the transitions from the serious to the trivial. Write down your reactions to the studio newsreaders and the reporters in the field—how do their

mannerisms and delivery affect the meaning of the news? Do you agree with Postman's criticisms?

2. Much to the amazement and dismay of many thinking people— such as Postman—former President Ronald Reagan was often called "The Great Communicator." Read something about Reagan's legendary communications skills. How did Reagan, who often bungled facts and could discuss few topics without cue cards, earn such a reputation? What other important elected position did Reagan hold?

3. Write an essay about the trend today to make history alive and real through theme parks, documentaries, and other forms of dramatization. Where must we draw the line between entertainment and distortion? Is it possible for most consumers to be sufficiently discerning to know what to believe and what to question? Is there value in giving half-accurate information versus no information at all?

Argument

A First Amendment Junkie

Susan Jacoby

*Susan Jacoby, a writer with impressive credentials, often fo-
cuses on women's issues. She has written for a broad range
of publications, including* The New York Times, The
Washington Post, *and the magazines* The Nation *and*
McCall's. *A collection of her essays was published in* The
Possible She *(1979). As you read this essay about pornography and feminism, published in 1978 in her* New York
Times *column, consider how her arguments would hold up
today.*

It is no news that many women are defecting from the ranks of civil
libertarians on the issue of obscenity. The conviction of Larry
Flynt, publisher of *Hustler* magazine—before his metamorphosis
into a born-again Christian—was greeted with unabashed feminist
approval. Harry Reems, the unknown actor who was convicted by a
Memphis jury for conspiring to distribute the movie *Deep Throat,* has
carried on his legal battles with almost no support from women who
ordinarily regard themselves as supporters of the First Amendment.
Feminist writers and scholars have even discussed the possibility of
making common cause against pornography with adversaries of the
women's movement—including opponents of the equal rights amendment and "right-to-life" forces.

All of this is deeply disturbing to a woman writer who believes, as
I always have and still do, in an absolute interpretation of the First
Amendment. Nothing in Larry Flynt's garbage convinces me that the
late Justice Hugo L. Black was wrong in this opinion that "the Federal
Government is without any power whatsoever under the Constitution

to put any type of burden on free speech and expression of ideas of any kind (as distinguished from conduct)." Many women I like and respect tell me I am wrong; I cannot remember having become involved in so many heated discussions of a public issue since the end of the Vietnam War. A feminist writer described my views as those of a "First Amendment junkie."

Many feminist arguments for controls on pornography carry the implicit conviction that porn books, magazines and movies pose a greater threat to women than similarly repulsive exercises of free speech pose to other offended groups. This conviction has, of course, been shared by everyone—regardless of race, creed or sex—who has ever argued in favor of abridging the First Amendment. It is the argument used by some Jews who have withdrawn their support from the American Civil Liberties Union because it has defended the right of American Nazis to march through a community inhabited by survivors of Hitler's concentration camps.

If feminists want to argue that the protection of the Constitution should not be extended to *any* particularly odious or threatening form of speech, they have a reasonable argument (although I don't agree with it). But it is ridiculous to suggest that the porn shops on 42d Street are more disgusting to women than a march of neo-Nazis is to survivors of the extermination camps.

5   The arguments over pornography also blur the vital distinction   5
between expression of ideas and conduct. When I say I believe unreservedly in the First Amendment, someone always comes back at me with the issue of "kiddie porn." But kiddie porn is not a First Amendment issue. It is an issue of the abuse of power—the power adults have over children—and not of obscenity. Parents and promoters have no more right to use their children to make porn movies than they do to send them to work in coal mines. The responsible adults should be prosecuted, just as adults who use children for back-breaking farm labor should be prosecuted.

Susan Brownmiller, in *Against Our Will: Men, Women and Rape,* has described pornography as "the undiluted essence of anti-female propaganda." I think this is a fair description of some types of pornography, especially of the brutish subspecies that equates sex with death and portrays women primarily as objects of violence.

The equation of sex and violence, personified by some glossy rock record album covers as well as by *Hustler,* has fed the illusion that censorship of pornography can be conducted on a more rational basis than other types of censorship. Are all pictures of naked women obscene? Clearly not, says a friend. A Renoir nude is art, she says, and *Hustler* is trash. "Any reasonable person" knows that.

But what about something between art and trash—something, say, along the lines of *Playboy* or *Penthouse* magazines? I asked five women for their reactions to one picture in *Penthouse* and got responses that ranged from "lovely" and "sensuous" to "revolting" and "demeaning." Feminists, like everyone else, seldom have rational reasons for their preferences in erotica. Like members of juries, they tend to disagree when confronted with something that falls short of 100 percent vulgarity.

In any case, feminists will not be the arbiters of good taste if it becomes easier to harass, prosecute and convict people on obscenity charges. Most of the people who want to censor girlie magazines are equally opposed to open discussion of issues that are of vital concern to women: rape, abortion, menstruation, contraception, lesbianism—in fact, the entire range of sexual experience from a woman's viewpoint.

Feminist writers and editors and film makers have limited financial resources: Confronted by a determined prosecutor, Hugh Hefner will fare better than Susan Brownmiller. Would the Memphis jurors who convicted Harry Reems for his role in *Deep Throat* be inclined to take a more positive view of paintings of the female genitalia done by sensitive feminist artists? *Ms.* magazine has printed color reproductions of some of those art works; *Ms.* is already banned from a number of high school libraries because someone considers it threatening and/or obscene.

Feminists who want to censor what they regard as harmful pornography have essentially the same motivation as other would-be censors: They want to use the power of the state to accomplish what they have been unable to achieve in the marketplace of ideas and images. The impulse to censor places no faith in the possibilities of democratic persuasion.

It isn't easy to persuade certain men that they have better uses for $1.95 each month than to spend it on a copy of *Hustler?* Well, then, give the men no choice in the matter.

I believe there is also a connection between the impulse toward censorship on the part of people who used to consider themselves civil libertarians and a more general desire to shift responsibility from individuals to institutions. When I saw the movie *Looking for Mr. Goodbar,* I was stunned by its series of visual images equating sex and violence, coupled with what seems to me the mindless message (a distortion of the fine Judith Rossner novel) that casual sex equals death. When I came out of the movie, I was even more shocked to see parents standing in line with children between the ages of 10 and 14.

I simply don't know why a parent would take a child to see such a movie, any more than I understand why people feel they can't turn off a television set their child is watching. Whenever I say that, my friends tell me I don't know how it is because I don't have children. True, but I do have parents. When I was a child, they did turn off the TV. They didn't expect the Federal Communications Commission to do their job for them.

15   I am a First Amendment junkie. You can't OD on the First 15
Amendment, because free speech is its own best antidote.

Questions on Meaning

1. What does Jacoby mean by her concluding statement, "free speech is its own best antidote"? Show how she supports this statement in the essay.
2. What does Jacoby intend you to conclude when she links Nazis and pornography? How does she use the American Civil Liberties Union's defense of American Nazis to support her argument against pornography censoring?
3. Jacoby feels that individuals who would censor pornography have the mind-set also to censor other forms of speech, including many of vital importance to women. What are some of the others Jacoby fears might be censored? What is the connection between pornography and these issues for these would-be censors?

Questions on Rhetorical Strategy and Style

1. Is Jacoby's argument based on facts and reasoning (logos), experiences and values (ethos), emotion and sympathy (pathos), or a combination of these elements? Find examples of each.
2. Jacoby and Susan Brownmiller, whom she quotes in the essay, disagree on the issue of censorship of pornography. How does Jacoby use the quotation from Brownmiller to strengthen her own argument?
3. Jacoby feels that censors want to "use the power of the state" to achieve their ends. Find where she uses example to argue against the intent of these censors.

Writing Assignments

1. Censorship has been used in recent years to restrict the distribution of information on abortion. Learn about restrictions placed on doctors and family planning advocates. Why and how have health-care providers been restricted? What impact has the censorship had? Where can patients go for information if their health-care providers are restricted? Organize your information into an informative essay.
2. The Internet has expanded the world of kiddie porn further than Jacoby—or almost anyone else—could have imagined in 1978, when this essay was written. Write an essay describing your

feelings about the availability of kiddie porn on the Internet. Argue why this material should or should not be censored.

3. What *does* constitute pornography? Is it purely visual or is it partly intent? Are, as Jacoby asks, "all pictures of naked women obscene"? What about naked men? When, where, and why is a nude vulgar and to whom? Write an essay defining pornography. As you define pornography, be sure to clarify your definition from other possible definitions.

The Right to Arms

Edward Abbey

Edward Abbey (1926–1989) was born in Pennsylvania but came west to attend the University of New Mexico. He lived most of his life in the Southwest, where he was a National Park Service ranger. He had a great love of the land and was angered by developers, polluters, and anyone who exploited natural resources. He wrote a number of novels, including Fire on the Mountain *(1963),* The Monkey Wrench Gang *(1975),* Good News *(1980), and* Hayduke Lives *(1991). His books of essays include* Desert Solitaire *(1968),* Abbey's Road *(1979), and* Down the River *(1982). The essay "The Right to Arms" comes from* Abbey's Road. *In it Abbey reveals his strong emotions about those who might try to take away our freedoms.*

If guns are outlawed
Only outlaws will have guns
(True? False? Maybe?)

1   Meaning weapons. The right to own, keep, and bear arms. A sword and a lance, or a bow and a quiverful of arrows. A crossbow and darts. Or in our time, a rifle and a handgun and a cache of ammunition. Firearms.

In medieval England a peasant caught with a sword in his possession would be strung up on a gibbet and left there for the crows. Swords were for gentlemen only. (*Gentlemen!*) Only members of the ruling class were entitled to own and bear weapons. For obvious reasons. Even bows and arrows were outlawed—see Robin Hood. When the peasants attempted to rebel, as they did in England and Germany and other European countries from time to time, they had to fight with sickles, bog hoes, clubs—no match for the sword-wielding armored cavalry of the nobility.

In Nazi Germany the possession of firearms by a private citizen of the Third Reich was considered a crime against the state; the statutory penalty was death—by hanging. Or beheading. In the Soviet Union, as in Czarist Russia, the manufacture, distribution, and ownership of firearms have always been monopolies of the state, strictly controlled and supervised. Any unauthorized citizen found with guns in his home by the OGPU or the KGB is automatically suspected of subversive intentions and subject to severe penalties. Except for the landowning aristocracy, who alone among the population were allowed the privilege of owning firearms, for only they were privileged to hunt, the ownership of weapons never did become a widespread tradition in Russia. And Russia has always been an autocracy—or at best, as today, an oligarchy.

In Uganda, Brazil, Iran, Paraguay, South Africa—wherever a few rule many—the possession of weapons is restricted to the ruling class and to their supporting apparatus: the military, the police, the secret police. In Chile and Argentina at this very hour men and women are being tortured by the most up-to-date CIA methods in the effort to force them to reveal the location of their hidden weapons. Their guns, their rifles. Their arms. And we can be certain that the Communist masters of modern China will never pass out firearms to *their* 800 million subjects. Only in Cuba, among dictatorships, where Fidel's revolution apparently still enjoys popular support, does there seem to exist a true citizen's militia.

There must be a moral in all this. When I try to think of a nation that has maintained its independence over centuries, and where the citizens still retain their rights as free and independent people, not many come to mind. I think of Switzerland. Of Norway, Sweden, Denmark, Finland. The British Commonwealth. France, Italy. And of our United States.

When Tell shot the apple from his son's head, he reserved in hand a second arrow, it may be remembered, for the Austrian tyrant Gessler. And got him too, shortly afterward. Switzerland has been a free country since 1390. In Switzerland basic national decisions are made by initiative and referendum—direct democracy—and in some cantons by open-air meetings in which all voters participate. Every Swiss male serves a year in the Swiss Army and at the end of the year takes his government rifle home with him—where he keeps it for the rest of his life. One of my father's grandfathers came from Canton Bern.

There must be a meaning in this. I don't think I'm a gun fanatic. I own a couple of small-caliber weapons, but seldom take them off the wall. I gave up deer hunting fifteen years ago, when the hunters began to outnumber the deer. I am a member of the National Rifle Association, but certainly no John Bircher. I'm a liberal—and proud of it. Nevertheless, I am opposed, absolutely, to every move the state makes to restrict my right to buy, own, possess, and carry a firearm. Whether shotgun, rifle, or handgun.

Of course, we can agree to a few commonsense limitations. Guns should not be sold to children, to the certifiably insane, or to convicted criminals. Other than that, we must regard with extreme suspicion any effort by the government—local, state, or national—to control our right to arms. The registration of firearms is the first step toward confiscation. The confiscation of weapons would be a major and probably fatal step into authoritarian rule—the domination of most of us by a new order of "gentlemen." By a new and harder oligarchy.

The tank, the B-52, the fighter-bomber, the state-controlled police and military are the weapons of dictatorship. The rifle is the weapon of democracy. Not for nothing was the revolver called an "equalizer." *Egalité* implies *liberté*. And always will. Let us hope our weapons are never needed—but do not forget what the common people of this nation knew when they demanded the Bill of Rights: An armed citizenry is the first defense, the best defense, and the final defense against tyranny.

If guns are outlawed, only the government will have guns. Only the police, the secret police, the military. The hired servants of our rulers. Only the government—and a few outlaws. I intend to be among the outlaws.

Questions on Meaning

1. Why is Abbey against gun control? State his thesis.
2. Does Abbey consider and argue against the reasons usually offered for gun control, such as the high number of murders committed with guns?

Questions on Rhetorical Strategy and Style

1. What examples does Abbey use to argue that gun control is linked to authoritarian government? Why doesn't he include examples of the many democratic countries, such as England, that curtail guns and yet have not given way to tyranny?
2. What are the strengths of Abbey's writing style? The weaknesses?
3. This essay argues against any laws to control guns. Considering the techniques of effective persuasion, evaluate Abbey's argument. Are you convinced? Why or why not?

Writing Assignments

1. Supposing there was a true "right" to own and carry any type of weapon, consider whether and how that right could or should be controlled. Compare this to other "rights" Americans enjoy: to drive our cars as we want, to drink alcohol and smoke cigarettes, to enjoy public places, and so on. What kinds of restrictions are there on these activities? How are they justified? Do you accept them or rebel against them? Write an essay in which you try to define a principle by which it is acceptable that government can regulate our freedoms in certain ways.
2. Abbey at one point refers to himself as a liberal, although typically the "liberals" are in favor of gun control measures and "conservatives" oppose them. Do some basic research into the meanings of liberal and conservative in modern politics. Write an essay in which you define both perspectives, and compare and contrast them in their general attitudes about the role of government (not specifically on the issue of gun control).

The Declaration of Independence

Thomas Jefferson

Thomas Jefferson (1743–1826) was born in Virginia in a well-to-do land-owning family. He graduated from the College of William and Mary and then studied law. When he was elected at age 26 to the Virginia legislature, he had already begun forming his revolutionary views. As a delegate to the Second Continental Congress in 1775, he was the principal writer of the Declaration of Independence, which was adopted on July 4, 1776. After the Revolution he was Governor of Virginia from 1775 to 1777. From then until 1801, when he was elected the third President of the United States, Jefferson served in various federal positions, including secretary of state and ambassador to France. Jefferson was influential as an advocate of democracy in the early years of the United States, although his ideas were more typical of the eighteenth century "enlightened man" than original. The Declaration of Independence shows his ideas and style as well as those of the times and remains not merely an important historical document but also an eloquent statement of the founding principles of this country.

1   When in the course of human events, it becomes necessary for one people to dissolve the political bands which have connected them with another, and to assume among the powers of the earth, the separate and equal station to which the Laws of Nature and of Nature's God entitle them, a decent respect to the opinions of mankind requires that they should declare the causes which impel them to the separation.

We hold these truths to be self-evident, that all men are created equal, that they are endowed by their Creator with certain inalienable rights, that among these are life, liberty, and the pursuit of happiness. That to secure these rights, governments are instituted among men, deriving their just powers from the consent of the governed. That whenever any form of government becomes destructive of these ends, it is the right of the people to alter or to abolish it, and to institute new government, laying its foundation on such principles and organizing its powers in such form, as to them shall seem most likely to effect their safety and happiness. Prudence, indeed, will dictate that governments long established should not be changed for light and transient causes; and accordingly all experience hath shown, that mankind are more disposed to suffer, while evils are sufferable, than to right themselves by abolishing the forms to which they are accustomed. But when a long train of abuses and usurpations, pursuing invariably the same object, evinces a design to reduce them under absolute despotism, it is their right, it is their duty, to throw off such government, and to provide new guards for their future security. Such has been the patient sufferance of these Colonies; and such is now the necessity which constrains them to alter their former systems of government. The history of the present King of Great Britain is a history of repeated injuries and usurpations, all having in direct object the establishment of an absolute tyranny over these States. To prove this, let facts be submitted to a candid world.

He has refused his assent to laws, the most wholesome and necessary for the public good.

He has forbidden his Governors to pass laws of immediate and pressing importance, unless suspended in their operation till his assent should be obtained; and when so suspended, he has utterly neglected to attend to them.

5   He has refused to pass other laws for the accommodation of large   5 districts of people, unless those people would relinquish the right of representation in the legislature, a right inestimable to them and formidable to tyrants only.

He has called together legislative bodies at places unusual, uncomfortable, and distant from the depository of their public records, for the sole purpose of fatiguing them into compliance with his measures.

He has dissolved representative houses repeatedly, for opposing with manly firmness his invasions on the rights of the people.

He has refused for a long time, after such dissolutions, to cause others to be elected; whereby the legislative powers, incapable of annihilation, have returned to the people at large for their exercise; the State remaining in the meantime exposed to all the dangers of invasion from without and convulsions within.

He has endeavoured to prevent the population of these states; for that purpose obstructing the laws for naturalization of foreigners; refusing to pass others to encourage their migration hither, and raising the conditions of new appropriations of lands.

10 He has obstructed the administration of justice, by refusing his assent to laws for establishing judiciary powers.

He has made judges dependent on his will alone, for the tenure of their offices, and the amount and payment of their salaries.

He has erected a multitude of new offices, and sent hither swarms of officers to harass our people, and eat out their substance.

He has kept among us, in times of peace, standing armies without the consent of our legislatures.

He has affected to render the military independent of and superior to the civil power.

15 He has combined with others to subject us to a jurisdiction foreign of our constitution, and unacknowledged by our laws; giving his assent to their acts of pretended legislation:

For quartering large bodies of armed troops among us:

For protecting them, by a mock trial, from punishment for any murders which they should commit on the inhabitants of these States:

For cutting off our trade with all parts of the world:

For imposing taxes on us without our consent:

20 For depriving us in many cases of the benefits of trial by jury:

For transporting us beyond seas to be tried for pretended offences:

For abolishing the free system of English laws in a neighbouring Province, establishing therein an arbitrary government, and enlarging its boundaries so as to render it at once an example and fit instrument for introducing the same absolute rule into these Colonies:

For taking away our Charters, abolishing our most valuable laws, and altering fundamentally the forms of our governments:

For suspending our own legislatures, and declaring themselves invested with power to legislate for us in all cases whatsoever.

25 He has abdicated government here, by declaring us out of his protection and waging war against us.

He has plundered our seas, ravaged our coasts, burnt our towns, and destroyed the lives of our people.

He is at this time transporting large armies of foreign mercenaries to complete the works of death, desolation, and tyranny, already begun with circumstances of cruelty and perfidy scarcely paralleled in the most barbarous ages, and totally unworthy the head of a civilized nation.

He has constrained our fellow citizens taken captive on the high seas to bear arms against their country, to become the executioners of their friends and brethren, or to fall themselves by their hands.

He has excited domestic insurrections amongst us, and has endeavoured to bring on the inhabitants of our frontiers, the merciless Indian savages, whose known rule of warfare, is an undistinguished destruction of all ages, sexes, and conditions.

30   In every stage of these oppressions we have petitioned for redress 30 in the most humble terms: our repeated petitions have been answered only by repeated injury. A prince whose character is thus marked by every act which may define a tyrant is unfit to be the ruler of a free people.

Nor have we been wanting in attention to our British brethren. We have warned them from time to time of attempts by their legislature to extend an unwarrantable jurisdiction over us. We have reminded them of the circumstances of our emigration and settlement here. We have appealed to their native justice and magnanimity, and we have conjured them by the ties of our common kindred to disavow these usurpations, which would inevitably interrupt our connections and correspondence. They too have been deaf to the voice of justice and of consanguinity. We must, therefore, acquiesce in the necessity, which denounces our separation, and hold them, as we hold the rest of mankind, enemies in war, in peace friends.

We, therefore, the Representatives of the United States of America, in General Congress assembled, appealing to the Supreme Judge of the world for the rectitude of our intentions, do, in the name, and by authority of the good people of these Colonies, solemnly publish and declare, That these United Colonies are, and of right ought to be, Free and Independent States; that they are absolved from all allegiance to the British Crown, and that all political connection between them and the state of Great Britain, is and ought to be totally dissolved; and that as Free and Independent States, they have full power to levy war, conclude peace, contract alliances, establish commerce, and to do all other acts and things which Independent States may of right do. And for the support of this declaration, with a firm reliance on the protection of Divine Providence, we mutually pledge to each other our lives, our fortunes, and our sacred honor.

Questions on Meaning

1. Most readers will recall the historical purpose of the Declaration of Independence, but unless you've had cause to read it in recent years you've probably forgotten much of its substance. As you just read it, what feelings did it evoke? What aspects had you forgotten? What is your impression of it now as a work of literature rather than as a historical document?
2. To whom is the Declaration of Independence addressed? What leads you to that conclusion?
3. Explain in your own words Jefferson's justification for democratic government.

Questions on Rhetorical Strategy and Style

1. The Declaration frequently uses dramatic language such as "sent hither swarms of officers to harass our people" and "plundered our seas, ravaged our coasts, burnt our towns, and destroyed the lives of our people." Find several other examples of similar powerful language. What is the purpose of such language in this document?
2. Note that the part of the Declaration that enumerates the long list of "facts . . . submitted to a candid world" comprises the greatest part of its length. Why is that?
3. Jefferson uses the rhetorical strategy of persuasion, to craft the Declaration. Identify at least two aspects of persuasion in this writing and explain their effect.

Writing Assignments

1. "Pursuit of happiness" is a phrase much used in the two centuries since it was written. Think about what that phrase implies about a government's power over people. Write an essay in which you define the right to pursue happiness in the modern world. Make sure you clarify with examples both what that right should guarantee and what it should not guarantee.
2. If the Colonies were justified in declaring their independence from what they saw as an oppressive England, were the Southern states also justified in declaring their independence when they seceded from the Union (thus beginning the Civil War)? Do some basic research if necessary to understand both situations, and then write an essay building your argument by comparing and contrasting these two situations.

Kiss Me, I'm Gay

Barbara Ehrenreich

Barbara Ehrenreich (1941–) was born in Montana and earned her Ph.D. from Rockefeller University. She is known as—and speaks of herself as—an independent and outspoken feminist, liberal, and democratic socialist. Most of her non-fiction writing could be classified as social criticism, including a number of books: The Hearts of Men *(1983),* Fear of Falling *(1989),* The Worst Years of Our Lives *(1990), and* Bait and Switch: The (Futile) Pursuit of the American Dream *(2005). Her* New York Times *best seller* Nickel and Dimed: On (Not) Getting By in America *(2001) exposed the reality of the working poor. Her novel,* Kipper's Game *was published in 1993. She is a regular essayist for* Time *magazine, where the essay "Kiss Me, I'm Gay" was first published in 1993. As an often controversial social critic, Ehrenreich frequently writes essays in which she tries to identify ways to correct problems or misunderstandings related to social issues. In the following essay, her real subject is not so much what it means to be gay as what society thinks about gays.*

1 A strange, unspoken assumption about human sexuality runs through the current debate on gay rights. Both sides agree, without saying so explicitly, that the human race consists of two types of people: heterosexuals and—on the other side of a great sexual dividing line—homosexuals. Heterosexuals are assumed to be the majority, while gays are thought to be a "minority," analogous to African Americans, Latinos, or any other ethnic group. Thus there is "gay pride" just as there is "black pride." We have Gay Pride marches just as we have Saint Patrick's Day or Puerto Rican Day parades. Gay militants even rallied, briefly, around the idea of a "queer nation."

There are ways in which this tribalistic view of human sexuality is useful and even progressive. Before the gay rights movement, homosexuality was conceived as a diffuse menace, attached to no partic-ular group and potentially threatening every man, at least in its "latent" form. So, naturally, as gays came out, they insisted on a unique and prideful group identity: We're queer and we're here! How else do you get ahead in America except by banding together and hoisting a flag?

Some studies seem to indicate that homosexuality is genetically based, more or less like left-handedness or being Irish. Heterosexuals, whether out of tolerance or spite, have been only too happy to con-cede to gays a special and probably congenital identity of their own. It's a way of saying: We're on this side of the great sexual divide—and you're on that.

There's only one problem with the theory of gays-as-ethnic-group: it denies the true plasticity of human sexuality and, in so doing, helps heterosexuals evade that which they really fear. And what het-erosexuals really fear is not that "they"—an alien subgroup with per-verse tastes in bedfellows—are getting an undue share of power and attention but that "they" might well be us.

5   Yes, certainly there are people who have always felt themselves to   5
be gay—or straight—since the first unruly fifth-grade crush or tickle in the groin. But for every study suggesting that homosexuality is in-nate, there are plenty of others that suggest human sexuality is far more versatile—or capricious, if you like. In his pioneering study, Al-fred Kinsey reported that 37 percent of the men and 19 percent of the women he surveyed acknowledged having had at least one orgasm with a partner of the same sex. William Masters and Virginia Johnson found that, among the people they studied, fantasies about sex with same-sex partners were the norm.

In some cultures, it is more or less accepted that "straight" men will nonetheless have sex with other men. The rapid spread of AIDS in Brazil, for example, is attributed to bisexual behavior on the part of os-tensibly heterosexual males. In the British upper class, homosexual ex-perience used to be a not uncommon feature of male adolescence. Young Robert Graves went off to World War I pining desperately for his schoolboy lover, but returned and eventually married. And, no, he did not spend his time in the trenches buggering his comrades-in-arms.

So being gay is not quite the same as being Irish. There are shad-ings; there are changes in the course of a lifetime. I know people who were once brazenly "out" and are now happily, heterosexually married—as well as people who have gone in the opposite direction. Or, to generalize beyond genital sexuality to the realm of affection and loyalty: we all know men who are militantly straight yet who reserve their deepest feelings for the male-bonded group—the team, the volunteer fire department, the men they went to war with.

The problem for the military is not that discipline will be undermined by a sudden influx of stereotypically swishy gays. The problem is that the military is still a largely unisexual institution—with all that that implies about the possibility of homosexual encounters. The traditionalists keep bringing up the "crowded showers," much like the dread unisex toilets of the ERA debate. But, from somewhere deep in the sexual imagination, the question inevitably arises: Why do they have such tiny, crowded showers anyway?

By saying that gays are a definite, distinguishable minority that can easily be excluded, the military may feel better about its own presumptive heterosexuality. But can "gays" really be excluded? Do eighteen-year-old recruits really have a firm idea what their sexuality is? The military could deal with its sexuality crisis much more simply, and justly, by ceasing to be such a unisexual institution and letting women in on an equal basis.

10   Perhaps we have all, "gays" and "straights," gotten as far as we can   10 with the metaphor of gays as a quasi-ethnic group, entitled to its own "rights." Perhaps it is time to acknowledge that the potential to fall in love with, or just be attracted to, a person of the same sex is widespread among otherwise perfectly conventional people. There would still be enormous struggle over what is right and wrong, "normal" and "abnormal." But at least this would be a struggle that everyone—gay or straight—would have a stake in: gays because of who they are; straights because of who they might be, and sometimes actually are. All men, for example, would surely be better off in a world where simple acts of affection between men occasioned no great commentary or suspicion. Where a hug would be a hug and not a "statement."

Questions on Meaning

1. What does Ehrenreich mean when she refers to a hug as a "statement"? Why would society view it that way?
2. The word "gay" is sometimes used to refer only to men, sometimes to include both gay men and lesbian women. We can tell through her examples and pronouns that Ehrenreich is writing strictly about men, not about lesbians. What do you make of this? Do you think she would say all of her points can be made equally well about lesbians—or is there something intrinsically different about gay men in terms of the ideas she writes about in this essay?
3. Ehrenreich mentions different research into the causes of gender identity and behavioral patterns, yet she seems not to argue in a cause and effect manner. Instead, her theme is about how society views and might better view gays. Why would it be better not to understand being gay the same way we understand being left-handed or being Irish?

Questions on Rhetorical Strategy and Style

1. Notice how the word "gay" is used in the last two paragraphs of the essay—sometimes inside quotation marks, sometimes not. Examine the pattern of word use here and explain that pattern in relation to what the essay says about what it means to be "gay."
2. Analyze how the essay develops from the first paragraph to the last. At what point does the thesis emerge clearly? Explain the advantages of having the thesis appear at that point, particularly in terms of how the essay builds to it and continues after it.
3. In much of her writing Ehrenreich interjects humor and frequently bold or outrageous figurative language. How would you characterize the tone of this piece? Comment on how the tone relates to the topic.

Writing Assignments

1. The researchers that Ehrenreich mentions have written much about the formation of sexual identity, and it is true that no one theory of the origins of sexual preference has emerged to account for the many variations in sexual identity and behavior. These researchers also write about the personal doubts and struggles most people have in establishing their own identity and becoming

comfortable with their own sexuality. This struggle is a major theme in literature, movies, and the theater. Choose a work you have read or seen recently in which a character has this struggle. Think about that character's difficulty—does it demonstrate that sexuality is not a simple either-or, black-or-white reality?

2. Ehrenreich makes a side point in this essay with this half-joking comment: "How else do you get ahead in America except by banding together and hoisting a flag?" On college campuses one often sees such groups forming in support of their particular causes. What have you observed in your own community or campus? Using familiar examples, write an essay looking at both the benefits and the disadvantages of this collective behavior to "get ahead."

3. Women have entered the military in increasing numbers, and society seems to be becoming more accepting of such "unisexual" institutions. On college campuses, too, there are often coed dormitories where not that long ago the sexes were strictly separated by locked doors and complicated check-in arrangements. Increasingly popular also are "unisex" bathrooms in places. Write an essay in which you explore this trend in breaking down traditional barriers, using additional examples you have observed.

What's Wrong with Gay Marriage?

Katha Pollitt

Katha Pollitt (1949–), a poet and essayist, was born in Brooklyn, New York and attended Radcliffe College (B.A., 1972). Pollitt, who has been an associate editor and columnist for The Nation, *has published in a number of other periodicals, including the* Atlantic Monthly, Mother Jones, The New York Times, *and* The New Yorker. *Her books include* Antarctic Traveler *(1982), a poetry compilation that received the National Book Critics Circle Award;* The Morning After: Sex, Fear, and Femininity on Campus *and* Reasonable Creatures: Essays on Women and Feminism *(1994). She also received a grant from the National Endowment for the Arts and a Guggenheim fellowship. In this essay from* The Nation, *Pollitt offers her pointed response to the controversy surrounding the decision by the Massachusetts Supreme Court granting gays the right to marriage.*

1   Will someone please explain to me how permitting gays and lesbians to marry threatens the institution of marriage? Now that the Massachusetts Supreme Court has declared gay marriage a constitutional right, opponents really have to get their arguments in line. The most popular theory, advanced by David Blankenhorn, Jean Bethke Elshtain and other social conservatives, is that under the tulle and orange blossom, marriage is all about procreation. There's some truth to this as a practical matter—couples often live together and tie the knot only when baby's on the way. But whether or not marriage is

the best framework for child rearing, having children isn't a marital requirement. As many have pointed out, the law permits marriage to the infertile, the elderly, the impotent and those with no wish to procreate; it allows married couples to use birth control, to get sterilized, to be celibate. There's something creepily authoritarian and insulting about reducing marriage to procreation, as if intimacy mattered less than biological fitness. It's not a view that anyone outside a right-wing think tank, a Catholic marriage tribunal or an ultra-Orthodox rabbi's court is likely to find persuasive.

So scratch procreation. How about: Marriage is the way women domesticate men. This theory, a favorite of right-wing writer George Gilder, has some statistical support—married men are much less likely than singles to kill people, crash the car, take drugs, commit suicide—although it overlooks such husbandly failings as domestic violence, child abuse, infidelity and abandonment. If a man rapes his wife instead of his date, it probably won't show up on a police blotter, but has civilization moved forward? Of course, this view of marriage as a barbarian-adoption program doesn't explain why women should undertake it—as is obvious from the state of the world, they haven't been too successful at it anyway. Nor does it explain why marriage should be restricted to heterosexual couples. The gay men and lesbians who want to marry don't impinge on the male improvement project one way or the other. Surely not even Gilder believes that a heterosexual pothead with plans for murder and suicide would be reformed by marrying a lesbian?

What about the argument from history? According to this, marriage has been around forever and has stood the test of time. Actually, though, marriage as we understand it—voluntary, monogamous, legally egalitarian, based on love, involving adults only—is a pretty recent phenomenon. For much of human history, polygyny was the rule—read your Old Testament—and in much of Africa and the Muslim world, it still is. Arranged marriages, forced marriages, child marriages, marriages predicated on the subjugation of women—gay marriage is like a fairy-tale romance compared with most chapters of the history of wedlock.

The trouble with these and other arguments against gay marriage is that they overlook how loose, flexible, individualized and easily dissolved the bonds of marriage already are. Virtually any man and woman can marry, no matter how ill assorted or little acquainted.

An eighty-year-old can marry an eighteen-year-old; a john can marry a prostitute; two terminally ill patients can marry each other from their hospital beds. You can get married by proxy, like medieval royalty, and not see each other in the flesh for years. Whatever may have been the case in the past, what undergirds marriage in most people's minds today is not some sociobiological theory about reproduction or male socialization. Nor is it the enormous bundle of privileges society awards to married people. It's love, commitment, stability.

5 Speaking just for myself, I don't like marriage. I prefer the old-fashioned ideal of monogamous free love, not that it worked out particularly well in my case. As a social mechanism, moreover, marriage seems to me a deeply unfair way of distributing social goods like health insurance and retirement checks, things everyone needs. Why should one's marital status determine how much you pay the doctor, or whether you eat cat food in old age, or whether a child gets a government check if a parent dies? It's outrageous that, for example, a working wife who pays Social Security all her life gets no more back from the system than if she had married a male worker earning the same amount and stayed home. Still, as long as marriage is here, how can it be right to deny it to those who want it? In fact, you would think that, given how many heterosexuals are happy to live in sin, social conservatives would welcome maritally minded gays with open arms. Gays already have the baby—they can adopt in many states, and lesbians can give birth in all of them—so why deprive them of the marital bathwater?

At bottom, the objections to gay marriage are based on religious prejudice: The marriage of man and woman is "sacred," and opening it to same-sexers violates its sacral nature. That is why so many people can live with civil unions but draw the line at marriage—spiritual union. In fact, polls show a striking correlation of religiosity, especially evangelical Protestantism, with opposition to gay marriage and with belief in homosexuality as a choice, the famous "gay lifestyle." For these people gay marriage is wrong because it lets gays and lesbians avoid turning themselves into the straights God wants them to be. As a matter of law, however, marriage is not about Adam and Eve versus Adam and Steve. It's not about what God blesses; it's about what the government permits. People may think *marriage* is a word wholly owned by religion, but actually it's wholly owned by the state. No matter how big your church wedding, you still have to get a marriage license from city hall. And just as divorced people can marry even if the Catholic Church considers it bigamy, and Muslim and Mormon men can marry only one woman even if their holy books tell them they can wed all the girls in Apartment 3G, two men or two women should be able to marry, even if religions oppose it and it makes some heterosexuals, raised in those religions, uncomfortable.

Gay marriage—it's not about sex, it's about separation of church and state.

Questions on Meaning

1. Besides the Massachusetts Supreme Court decision, why has gay marriage become such a controversial topic recently?
2. What definitions of marriage does Pollitt offer in her article and what are the assumptions behind each? Which definition most captures your own beliefs about marriage?
3. According to the author, why is gay marriage not a matter of sex, but a matter of separation of church and state?

Questions on Rhetorical Strategy and Style

1. The article opens with a question. How is the reader supposed to respond to it?
2. Why does the author review several assumptions about the basis for marriage before revealing her agenda in paragraph four?
3. In the same paragraph, Pollitt characterizes marriage as an already unstable institution. How does this strategy serve or undermine her argument?

Writing Assignments

1. The article ends with the assertion that gay marriage is not a sexual issue but a constitutional one. In a brief essay, explain why you agree or disagree with this proposition. What social conditions suggest the quandary of the gay marriage issue?
2. Many who oppose gay marriage support the concept of civil unions. Write an essay in which you postulate on the political, legal, and moral reasons for this seemingly contradictory stance.

It's Time to Get Serious
Theodore Dalrymple

Theodore Dalrymple is the pen name of Anthony Daniels (1949–), born in England to a communist activist and a refugee from Nazi Germany. After graduating from Birmingham Medical School in England in 1974, he practiced medicine and psychiatry in Tanzania and Zimbabwe, as well as in British prisons and inner-city hospitals. Dalrymple has been writing a column for the London Spectator *since the early 1990s. He is also a contributing editor for* The City Journal, *a publication of the Manhattan Institute, where he serves as a Dietrich Weismann Fellow. A vocal opponent of progressive and liberal political philosophies, Dalrymple appears regularly in conservative publications such as* The National Review *and on radio programs such as "Radio Live with Phyllis Schlafly," "Fox Forum," and "The Donovan Report." Dalrymple's work has earned him the sobriquet "Orwell of our time," a title conferred on him by* Arts & Letters Daily *editor Denis Dutton. His books include* Life at the Bottom: The Worldview that Makes the Underclass *(2001) and* Our Culture, What's Left of It: The Mandarins and the Masses *(2005). In this essay from* The Spectator *Dalrymple takes a controversial stand on the violent Muslim protests against the Danish cartoons, arguing that the lack of response from the West is nothing short of cowardly.*

1 When the Taleban blew up the ancient statues of Buddha in Afghanistan, there were no spontaneous or state-sponsored demonstrations in the Islamic world demanding that the feelings of Buddhists should be spared. Furthermore, the cartoonists

and commentators of the Middle East have never been sparing with their insults of other people or of other people's beliefs.

In Egypt, one of the more tolerant of Middle Eastern countries, *The Protocols of the Elders of Zion*[1] is available everywhere on the streets, often with accompanying caricatures straight out of Der Sturmer. My copy of *The Protocols* was printed and published in Kuwait, in a series devoted to Islamic philosophy for students, complete with a preface asserting its authenticity, as proof of which the endorsement of the *Times* in 1920 was quoted, but not the almost immediate retraction after further investigation by a writer on the *Times* conclusively demonstrated that *The Protocols* was an egregious forgery.

Furthermore, open intellectual criticism of Islam is not welcomed in Muslim countries. A man who stood up in public and stated in a Muslim country that there is no God and Mohammed was not his prophet would be suspected of suicidal tendencies. Ibn Warraq's detailed and scholarly rejection of Islam, entitled "Why I Am Not a Muslim," is not available anywhere in the Muslim world, though it treats of a subject of supreme importance for that world, namely the intellectual basis and justification, or lack of it, of the faith. Not only did the author have to assume a false name, but he cannot now safely live in a Muslim country. Whether this would have been so 800 years ago, during the golden age of Islamic (relative) tolerance and intellectual activity, is quite beside the point: it is so now, and that is what counts.

But the deficiencies and less attractive aspects of Islamic philosophy, society and practice are sufficiently well known to require no rehearsal. We hardly need to be told again that Islam fails to make a proper distinction between Church and state, that it has had no Reformation or Enlightenment, that it regards all non-Muslims as inferiors, that it has produced nothing of universal human intellectual or cultural significance for three or four hundred years, and so forth. We should rather take the opportunity to look at ourselves.

5   What does the episode tell us about ourselves? The first is that we   5 are not morally serious people; in a word, that we are decadent. In this sense, the Muslim world is quite right about us. It correctly perceives cowardice, weakness and absence of any deep belief in the principles we supposedly espouse.

You would not have to be an acute psychologist, for example, to descry the insincerity and fear in the expressions of sympathy for

Muslim outrage emanating from both British and American governments. It is abject nonsense to say that we understand and even share to some degree the primitive Muslim outrage expressed–belatedly, and often with state encouragement–at the Danish cartoons, in the unctuous Clintonian sense of feeling their pain. Perhaps we understand the outrage in the anthropological sense, as a symptom of injured pride and the thuggishness that injured pride generates. But that is not what Jack Straw,[2] the Neville Chamberlain de nos jours, meant, or rather intended us to think he meant.

We do not, most of us, respect Islam any more than we respect people who speak in tongues. What we respect is the right of Muslims to practise their religion in perfect peace, in so far as it does not conflict with our laws. We also hope that we can find common ground with them in many other aspects of human existence: in business, in the professions, in literature and so forth. Tolerance is not a matter of respecting what is tolerated–if it were, tolerance would hardly be necessary. Tolerance is the willing, conscious suppression of distaste or disdain for other people's ideas, habits and tastes for the sake of a wider social peace.

Surely Muslims in this country and elsewhere know perfectly well that we, most of us, do not respect their religion, in the sense of according it high intellectual, moral or artistic status in the modern world (the past is another matter, as a visit to the Victoria & Albert Museum, for example, will quickly confirm). Some among them find this intolerable, and therefore demand the kind of respect that young men of Jamaican descent and criminal propensities demand, knowing full well that such respect is indistinguishable from fear.

Again, you would not have to be a very acute psychologist to detect the fear in Mr. Straw's craven remarks, in the abject apologies of the Danes (who have nothing to apologise for) and in the statements emanating from the American government. Our government evidently finds it easier, or more politically expedient, to bomb distant countries than to face up to thugs a few hundred yards away.

10 The reaction of Britain and the United States will have taught 10 Muslim extremists that if they are thuggish enough, they can intimidate powerful states, and that professions of belief in freedom of expression are hollow; in other words, that the terrorist tactics of the weak can impose censorship on the strong. Muslim extremists will have come to the not altogether mistaken conclusion that the men

who control Western governments don't believe in anything strongly enough to risk their own skins; in short, that they are decadent.

Instead, Muslims should be told quite clearly that our citizens have the legal right to criticise, lampoon, ridicule and mock Mohammed to their heart's content, in any way that they wish: that Islam and Muslims have no special claim to protection from the rough and tumble of post-Enlightenment intellectual, political and social life. If they cannot live in a society in which this is the case, they should go somewhere else; they are, after all, spoilt for choice, at least in theory.

Of course, a right does not imply a duty to exercise it, and there are many reasons for doing things, or for not doing them, other than that there is a right to do them or not do them. Surely we are all familiar with the duty to censor ourselves with a view to smoothing social relations and not causing unnecessary and pointless distress to others. I have long since given up arguing with people who hold beliefs that I consider ridiculous, provided only that they are not trying to impose them on me. There is much to be said for polite silence—indeed a truly tolerant society requires many such silences.

Unfortunately, the thuggery that we have seen recently—with enraged demonstrators openly calling for murders, decapitations and holocausts, under the disgraceful, pusillanimous and cowardly protection of the police—renders such polite silence indistinguishable from cowardice. A tolerant society cannot survive if it turns a blind eye to people who insist on being intolerable. By their behaviour the Muslim extremists are in danger of making scurrility and disrespect towards Islam a positive duty of free men and women.

But the loss of tolerance in our society does not come entirely from malign outside forces. We have lost the appreciation that tolerance requires silence on many matters, and that our instinct to brush things under the carpet is often a sound and civilised one. We have also lost an appreciation that freedom requires restraint, if men are to live in society.

15 It is well that we should try to see ourselves as others see us. 15 I have read some of the criticisms by Muslims of Western society, and many of them seem to me to be justified. The lack of public dignity, the licence, the open and triumphant vulgarity are indeed deeply unattractive, as any real conservative would surely understand, but our Conservative party is too cowardly ever to admit as much. It is

scarcely any wonder that Muslim commentators see Western freedom as little more than a desire to incontinently enjoy ourselves in ever more gross and sensational ways: a desire that is self-defeating and leads to a great deal of misery, as well as social breakdown.

Of course, Islam has no answer to the problem beyond repression and theocratic tyranny, which are guarantees of a different kind of misery and social breakdown. In general, Muslim commentators do not understand the connection between Western power and Western freedom, including religious freedom. If they did, they would have to reject some of the pretensions of Islam, and thus open themselves up to criticism from the more-Islamic-than-thou brigade: a perennial problem for Muslims.

But we ourselves have experienced a loss of moral understanding and subtlety. For example, the word 'transgressive' is often used as a term of approbation of a work of art, as if we could conceive of nothing that should not be transgressed, or of a taboo that should not be broken. This is not a call to abject conventionality: it is a call to moral seriousness rather than the frivolity that has unnecessarily brought about so many of the unattractive features of our prosperous modernity.

As it happens, the Danish cartoons were making a morally serious point, if not very well; which is why, of course, they provoked such outrage. It is a sign of our moral frivolity that we have failed to defend and protect the Danes with the utmost vigour, without equivocation, on a point of the most profound principle. Their freedom is our freedom; and we should not forget that it is but a short step, morally and historically, from Chamberlain to Petain.[3]

End Notes

1. *The Protocols of the Elders of Zion:* A forged document claiming to be the blueprint for a secret Jewish conspiracy to dominate the world.
2. Jack Straw: The leaders of the British House of Commons. Neville Chamberlain: British Prime Minister whose policy of appeasement emboldened Adolf Hitler prior to the outbreak of world War II. *De nos jours* (French) in our time.
3. Petain: French military hero from World War I who headed the Vichy government in collaboration with the Nazi occupiers of Franch during World War II.

Questions on Meaning

1. How does Dalrymple characterize contemporary Islam? What distinctions does he make (if any) between radical and traditional Islamic philosophy?
2. Why does Dalrymple label Western sympathy for Muslim outrage over the Danish cartoons "abject nonsense"?
3. What are the broader implications, according to Dalrymple, of the West's response to the violent protests over the cartoons?

Questions on Rhetorical Strategy and Style

1. In order to persuade, a writer must present him- or herself as credible and sympathetic. In your view, does Dalrymple accomplish this? Explain your response.
2. What points of contrast between Muslim thought and Western thought does Dalrymple highlight? How do these contrasts contribute to his argument?
3. Essential to any argument is careful definition of terms. How does Dalrymple define terms such as *decadent* and *tolerance?* Identify several other essential terms in the article, and explain how Dalrymple defines them.

Writing Assignments

1. Write a letter to the editor of *The Spectator* in response to Dalrymple's argument. Explain in your letter why you support or reject his position.
2. Research the reaction to the Danish cartoons in the Islamic world and among Muslims in Western countries. Then write a report on the reaction, highlighting the variety of ways in which Muslim clerics, governments, and individuals dealt with the controversy.

I Have a Dream

Martin Luther King, Jr.

Martin Luther King, Jr. (1929–1968) was born in At-
lanta, Georgia, the son and grandson of Baptist ministers.
His college and postgraduate studies took him from Moor-
house College to Crozer Theological Seminary to Boston
University, where he received a Ph.D. (1955) and met his
future wife, Coretta Scott. King's active involvement in the
civil rights movement began in 1955, when he led a boy-
cott of segregated buses in Montgomery, Alabama. From the
mid-1950s until he was shot and killed in Memphis, Ten-
nessee, while supporting striking city workers, King orga-
nized boycotts, sit-ins, mass demonstrations, and other
protest activities. As a black civil rights leader, King was ar-
rested, jailed, stoned, stabbed, and beaten; his house was
bombed; and he was placed under secret surveillance by
Federal Bureau of Investigation (FBI) director J. Edgar
Hoover. Through his leadership—always underscored by his
nonviolent beliefs—King's name has become synonymous
with the watersheds of the civil rights movement in the
United States: Rosa Parks, the Southern Christian Leader-
ship Conference, Selma, Alabama, the Civil Rights Act,
and the Voting Rights Act. His crowning moment occurred
during the August 1963 civil rights march on Washington,
D.C., when King, standing in front of the Lincoln Memo-
rial, delivered his most famous speech, this essay. A year later
he would receive the Nobel Peace Prize. As you read King's
words, spoken nearly a century after Lincoln signed the
Emancipation Proclamation, listen to this great orator; try
to feel the emotion that hundreds of thousands of black
Americans carried to the Esplanade that memorable day.

1   I am happy to join with you today in what will go down in history   1
as the greatest demonstration for freedom in the history of our
nation.

Five score years ago, a great American, in whose symbolic shadow
we stand today, signed the Emancipation Proclamation. This mo-
mentous decree came as a great beacon light of hope to millions of
Negro slaves who had been seared in the flames of withering injustice.
It came as a joyous daybreak to end the long night of their captivity.
But one hundred years later, the Negro is still not free. One hundred
years later, the life of the Negro is still sadly crippled by the manacles
of segregation and the chains of discrimination. One hundred years
later, the Negro lives on a lonely island of poverty in the midst of a
vast ocean of material prosperity. One hundred years later, the Negro
is still anguished in the corners of American society and finds himself
in exile in his own land. And so we have come here today to dramatize a shameful condition.

In a sense we have come to our nation's capital to cash a check.
When the architects of our republic wrote the magnificent words of
the Constitution and the Declaration of Independence, they were
signing a promissory note to which every American was to fall heir.
This note was the promise that all men—yes, Black men as well as
white men—would be guaranteed the inalienable rights of life, liberty,
and the pursuit of happiness.

It is obvious today that America has defaulted on this promissory
note insofar as her citizens of color are concerned. Instead of honoring
this sacred obligation, America has given the Negro people a bad check,
a check which has come back marked "insufficient funds." But we
refuse to believe that the bank of justice is bankrupt. We refuse to believe that there are insufficient funds in the great vaults of opportunity
of this nation; and so we have come to cash this check, a check that will
give us upon demand the riches of freedom and the security of justice.

5   We have also come to this hallowed spot to remind America of   5
the fierce urgency of *now*. This is no time to engage in the luxury of
cooling off or to take the tranquilizing drug of gradualism. Now is the
time to make real the promises of democracy. Now is the time to rise
from the dark and desolate valley of segregation to the sunlit patch of
racial justice. Now is the time to lift our nation from the quicksands
of racial injustice to the solid rock of brotherhood. Now is the time to
make justice a reality for all of God's children.

It would be fatal for the nation to overlook the urgency of the moment. This sweltering summer of the Negro's legitimate discontent will not pass until there is an invigorating autumn of freedom and equality. Nineteen Sixty-three is not an end, but a beginning. And those who hope that the Negro needed to blow off steam and will now be content will have a rude awakening if the nation returns to business as usual. There will be neither rest nor tranquility in America until the Negro is granted his citizenship rights. The whirlwinds of revolt will continue to shake the foundations of our nation until the bright day of justice emerges.

But there is something that I must say to my people who stand on the warm threshold which leads into the palace of justice. In the process of gaining our rightful place, we must not be guilty of wrongful deeds. Let us not seek to satisfy our thirst for freedom by drinking from the cup of bitterness and hatred. We must forever conduct our struggle on the high plane of dignity and discipline. We must not allow our creative protest to degenerate into physical violence. Again and again we must rise to the majestic heights of meeting physical force with soul force. And the marvelous new militancy which has engulfed the Negro community must not lead us to a distrust of all white people; for many of our white brothers, as evidenced by their presence here today, have come to realize that their destiny is tied up with our destiny, and they have come to realize that their freedom is inextricably bound to our freedom.

We cannot walk alone. And as we walk we must make the pledge that we shall always march ahead. We cannot turn back. There are those who are asking the devotees of civil rights, "When will you be satisfied?" We can never be satisfied as long as the Negro is the victim of the unspeakable horrors of police brutality. We can never be satisfied as long as our bodies, heavy with the fatigue of travel, cannot gain lodging in the motels of the highways and the hotels of the cities. We cannot be satisfied as long as the Negro's basic mobility is from a smaller ghetto to a larger one. We can never be satisfied as long as our children are stripped of their selfhood and robbed of their dignity by signs stating "For Whites Only." We cannot be satisfied as long as the Negro in Mississippi cannot vote and a Negro in New York believes he has nothing for which to vote. No, no, we are not satisfied, and we will not be satisfied until justice rolls down like waters and righteousness like a mighty stream.

I am not unmindful that some of you have come here out of great trials and tribulations. Some of you have come fresh from narrow jail cells. Some of you have come from areas where your quest for freedom left you battered by the storms of persecution and staggered by the winds of police brutality. You have been the veterans of creative suffering. Continue to work with the faith that unearned suffering is redemptive.

10   Go back to Mississippi, and go back to Alabama. Go back to   10
South Carolina. Go back to Georgia. Go back to Louisiana. Go back to the slums and ghettos of our Northern cities, knowing that somehow this situation can and will be changed. Let us not wallow in the valley of despair.

I say to you today, my friends, even though we face the difficulties of today and tomorrow, I still have a dream. It is a dream deeply rooted in the American dream. I have a dream that one day this nation will rise up and live out the true meaning of its creed: "We hold these truths to be self-evident, that all men are created equal." I have a dream that one day, on the red hills of Georgia, sons of former slaves and the sons of former slave owners will be able to sit down together at the table of brotherhood. I have a dream that one day even the state of Mississippi, a state sweltering with the heat of injustice, sweltering with the heat of oppression, will be transformed into an oasis of freedom and justice. I have a dream that my four little children will one day live in a nation where they will not be judged by the color of their skin, but by the content of their character.

I have a dream today. I have a dream that one day down in Alabama—with its vicious racists, with its governor's lips dripping with the words of interposition and nullification—one day right there in Alabama, little Black boys and Black girls will be able to join hands with little white boys and white girls as sisters and brothers.

I have a dream today. I have a dream that one day every valley shall be exalted and every hill and mountain shall be made low, the rough places will be made plain and the crooked places will be made straight, and the glory of the Lord shall be revealed, and all flesh shall see it together.

This is our hope. This is the faith that I go back to the South with. And with this faith we will be able to hew out of the mountain of despair a stone of hope. With this faith we will be able to transform the jangling discords of our nation into a beautiful symphony of brotherhood. With this faith we will be able to work together, to play together, to struggle together, to go to jail together, to stand up for freedom together, knowing that we will be free one day.

15   And this will be the day—this will be the day when all of God's 15 children will be able to sing with new meaning.

> *My country, 'tis of thee,*
> *Sweet land of liberty,*
>   *Of thee I sing;*
> *Land where my fathers died,*
> *Land of the Pilgrims' pride,*
> *From every mountainside*
> *Let freedom ring.*

And if America is to be a great nation, this must become true.

And so let freedom ring from the prodigious hilltops of New Hampshire. Let freedom ring from the mighty mountains of New York. Let freedom ring from the heightening Alleghenies of Pennsylvania. Let freedom ring from the snow-capped Rockies of Colorado. Let freedom ring from the curvaceous slopes of California.

But not only that. Let freedom ring from Stone Mountain of Georgia. Let freedom ring from Lookout Mountain of Tennessee. Let freedom ring from every hill and molehill of Mississippi. "From every mountainside let freedom ring."

And when this happens—when we allow freedom to ring, when we let it ring from every village and every hamlet, from every state and every city—we will be able to speed up that day when all of God's children, Black men and white men, Jews and Gentiles, Protestants and Catholics, will be able to join hands and sing in the words of the old Negro spiritual: "Free at last! Free at last! Thank God Almighty. We are free at last!"

Questions on Meaning

1. King presents two primary reasons for the civil rights march on Washington, D.C., during which he delivered this speech—a "shameful condition" in America and a "fierce urgency" for black Americans. Without looking at the essay, describe the shameful condition and explain the urgency of which King speaks.

2. King stated that the marchers had gone to Washington "to cash a check" because black Americans had not received their due from the Constitution and Declaration of Independence. Is this because these documents were not strong enough or because they were not applied equitably? Select a major incident during the civil rights movement—such as the integration of the University of Mississippi—and try to determine whether weak laws or weak enforcement denied black Americans the same rights as white Americans.

3. King's stalwart belief in nonviolence (note paragraph 7), his rich Christian background, and his irrepressible optimism flow through this essay. Although he cites years of injustice, nevertheless he weaves a thread of hope. Find two examples of King's hope for the future. In hindsight, was his hope justified?

Questions on Rhetorical Strategy and Style

1. Were you captivated by King's metaphors, or did any of them interfere with your reading? Look back through the essay and list metaphors that worked for you and those that did not. Consider that in many cases the effects could be different for you now than for King's original audience. Rewrite the metaphors that you feel were ineffective.

2. Like many orators, King employs repetition to help persuade his audience. Locate three examples of repetition and rewrite those passages without the repetitive phraseology. How does it affect the impact of King's words?

3. Reread the essay. As you read, note the ebb and flow of King's words, his constant use of metaphors, his repetition of key phrases. Does his preacher's style interfere with the message? Next, reread the essay again, but this time stand up, face an imaginary audience of a quarter million emotion-charged supporters, and read the oration *aloud.* Compare your reaction to King's rhetorical style when you read the essay aloud to when you read it silently. How does an essay's manner of delivery affect how it is written?

Writing Assignments

1. Consider the socioeconomic landscape of America today. Identify a minority group in the United States (by ethnicity, gender, income, etc.) and imagine a different version of the "I Have a Dream" essay presented to a gathering of members of this group. How might this speech be different from King's?
2. King delivered his "I Have a Dream" speech in the early 1960s, but many Americans would say that it still has relevance today. Have black Americans achieved King's dream? Have King's words had the impact attributed to them? Write an essay on the relevance of this speech today, supporting your arguments with clear examples.
3. Have you ever experienced an injustice, such as racial, sexual, or age discrimination? Do you know someone who has? Write an essay describing this injustice. Describe the situation, why it was unjust, how you or your acquaintance felt, and what was done. Use various rhetorical strategies, such as comparison and contrast, description, and example to substantiate your argument.

Letter from Birmingham Jail

Martin Luther King, Jr.

Martin Luther King, Jr. (1929–1968) was born in Atlanta, Georgia. The son and grandson of Baptist ministers, he attended Moorhouse College, Crozer Theological Seminary, and Boston University where he received a Ph.D. (1955) and met his future wife, Coretta Scott. King's active involvement in the civil rights movement began in 1955, when he led a boycott of segregated buses in Montgomery, Alabama. From the mid 1950s until he was shot and killed in Memphis, Tennessee, while supporting striking city workers, King organized boycotts, sit-ins, mass demonstrations, and other protest activities. As a black civil rights leader, King was arrested, jailed, stoned, stabbed, and beaten; his house was bombed; he was placed under secret surveillance by Federal Bureau of Investigation (FBI) director J. Edgar Hoover; and in 1966 he was awarded the Nobel Peace Prize. Through his leadership—always underscored by his nonviolent beliefs—King's name has become synonymous with the watersheds of the civil rights movement in the United States: Rosa Parks; the Southern Christian Leadership Conference (which King founded); Selma, Alabama; the Civil Rights Act; the Voting Rights Act; and the 1963 civil rights march on Washington, D. C. His published works include Strength to Love *(1963) and* Conscience for Change *(1967). This essay—published in a revised form in* Why We Can't Wait *(1964)—is King's stern response to eight clergymen from Alabama who were asking civil rights activists to give up public demonstrations in Birmingham, Alabama, and*

---

turn to the courts. Read the clergymen's public statement first, then King's detailed rebuttal (printed here as it appeared originally). Keep in mind that King wrote these words four months before he delivered his famous "I Have a Dream" speech during the August 1963 civil rights march on Washington; after long years of activism, he was clearly impatient with the slow progress of the civil rights movement.

Public Statement by Eight Alabama Clergymen

(April 12, 1963)

We the undersigned clergymen are among those who, in January, issued "An Appeal for Law and Order and Common Sense," in dealing with racial problems in Alabama. We expressed understanding that honest convictions in racial matters could properly be pursued in the courts, but urged that decisions of those courts should in the meantime be peacefully obeyed.

Since that time there had been some evidence of increased forbearance and a willingness to face facts. Responsible citizens have undertaken to work on various problems which cause racial friction and unrest. In Birmingham, recent public events have given indication that we all have opportunity for a new constructive and realistic approach to racial problems.

However, we are now confronted by a series of demonstrations by some of our Negro citizens, directed and led in part by outsiders. We recognize the natural impatience of people who feel that their hopes are slow in being realized. But we are convinced that these demonstrations are unwise and untimely.

We agree rather with certain local Negro leadership which has called for honest and open negotiation of racial issues in our area. And we believe this kind of facing of issues can best be accomplished by citizens of our own metropolitan area, white and Negro, meeting with their knowledge and experience of the local situation. All of us need to face that responsibility and find proper channels for its accomplishment.

5   Just as we formerly pointed out that "hatred and violence have no   5
sanction in our religious and political traditions," we also point out
that such actions as incite to hatred and violence, however technically
peaceful those actions may be, have not contributed to the resolution
of our local problems. We do not believe that these days of new hope
are days when extreme measures are justified in Birmingham.

We commend the community as a whole, and the local news
media and law enforcement officials in particular, on the calm manner in which these demonstrations have been handled. We urge the
public to continue to show restraint should the demonstrations continue, and the law enforcement officials to remain calm and continue
to protect our city from violence.

We further strongly urge our own Negro community to withdraw
support from these demonstrations, and to unite locally in working
peacefully for a better Birmingham. When rights are consistently denied, a cause should be pressed in the courts and in negotiations
among local leaders, and not in the streets. We appeal to both our
white and Negro citizenry to observe the principles of law and order ·
and common sense.

Signed by:

C.C. J. CARPENTER, D.D., LL.D., *Bishop of Alabama*
JOSEPH A. DURICK, D.D., *Auxiliary Bishop, Diocese of
     Mobile, Birmingham*
RABBI MILTON L. GRAFMAN, *Temple Emanu-El,
     Birmingham, Alabama*
BISHOP PAUL HARDIN, *Bishop of the Alabama-West Florida
     Conference of the Methodist Church*
BISHOP NOLAN B. HARMON, *Bishop of the North Alabama
     Conference of the Methodist Church*
GEORGE M. MURRAY, D.D., LL.D., *Bishop Coadjutor,
     Episcopal Diocese of Alabama*
EDWARD V. RAMAGE, *Moderator, Synod of the Alabama
     Presbyterian Church in the United States*
EARL STALLINGS, *Pastor, First Baptist Church, Birmingham,
     Alabama*

Letter from Birmingham Jail

MARTIN LUTHER KING, JR.
Birmingham City Jail
April 16, 1963

Bishop C. C. J. Carpenter
Bishop Joseph A. Durick
Rabbi Milton L. Grafman
Bishop Paul Hardin
Bishop Nolan B. Harmon
The Rev. George M. Murray
The Rev. Edward V. Ramage
The Rev. Earl Stallings

My dear Fellow Clergymen,

While confined here in the Birmingham City Jail, I came across your recent statement calling our present activities "unwise and untimely." Seldom, if ever, do I pause to answer criticism of my work and ideas. If I sought to answer all of the criticisms that cross my desk, my secretaries would be engaged in little else in the course of the day and I would have no time for constructive work. But since I feel that you are men of genuine good will and your criticisms are sincerely set forth, I would like to answer your statement in what I hope will be patient and reasonable terms.

I think I should give the reason for my being in Birmingham, since you have been influenced by the argument of "outsiders coming in." I have the honor of serving as president of the Southern Christian Leadership Conference, an organization operating in every Southern state with headquarters in Atlanta, Georgia. We have some eighty-five affiliate organizations all across the South—one being the Alabama Christian Movement for Human Rights. Whenever necessary and possible we share staff, educational, and financial resources with our affiliates. Several months ago our local affiliate here in Birmingham invited us to be on call to engage in a nonviolent direct action program if such were deemed necessary. We readily consented, and when the hour came we lived up to our promises. So I, along with several members of my staff, am here, because I was invited here. I am here because I have basic organizational ties here.

But more basically, I am in Birmingham because injustice is here. Just as the eighth century prophets left their little villages and carried their "thus saith the Lord" far beyond the boundaries of their home town, and just as the Apostle Paul left his little village of Tarsus and carried the gospel of Jesus Christ to practically every hamlet and city of the Greco-Roman world, I too am compelled to carry the gospel of freedom beyond my particular home town. Like Paul, I must constantly respond to the Macedonian call for aid.

Moreover, I am cognizant of the interrelatedness of all communities and states. I cannot sit idly by in Atlanta and not be concerned about what happens in Birmingham. Injustice anywhere is a threat to justice everywhere. We are caught in an inescapable network of mutuality, tied in a single garment of destiny. Whatever affects one directly affects all indirectly. Never again can we afford to live with the narrow, provincial "outside agitator" idea. Anyone who lives inside the United States can never be considered an outsider anywhere in this country.

You deplore the demonstrations that are presently taking place in Birmingham. But I am sorry that your statement did not express a similar concern for the conditions that brought the demonstrations into being. I am sure that each of you would want to go beyond the superficial social analyst who looks merely at effects, and does not grapple with underlying causes. I would not hesitate to say that it is unfortunate that so-called demonstrations are taking place in Birmingham at this time, but I would say in more emphatic terms that it is even more unfortunate that the white power structure of this city left the Negro community with no other alternative.

In any nonviolent campaign there are four basic steps: (1) collection of the facts to determine whether injustices are alive; (2) negotiation; (3) self-purification; and (4) direct action. We have gone through all of these steps in Birmingham. There can be no gainsaying of the fact that racial injustice engulfs this community. Birmingham is probably the most thoroughly segregated city in the United States. Its ugly record of police brutality is known in every section of this country. Its unjust treatment of Negroes in the courts is a notorious reality. There have been more unsolved bombings of Negro homes and churches in Birmingham than any city in this nation. These are the hard, brutal, and unbelievable facts. On the basis of these conditions, Negro leaders sought to negotiate with the city fathers. But the political leaders consistently refused to engage in good faith negotiation.

Then came the opportunity last September to talk with some of the leaders of the economic community. In these negotiating sessions certain promises were made by the merchants—such as the promise to remove the humiliating racial signs from the stores. On the basis of these promises Rev. Shuttlesworth and the leaders of the Alabama Christian Movement for Human Rights agreed to call a moratorium on any type of demonstrations. As the weeks and months unfolded we realized that we were the victims of a broken promise. The signs remained. As in so many experiences of the past we were confronted with blasted hopes, and the dark shadow of a deep disappointment settled upon us. So we had no alternative except that of preparing for direct action, whereby we would present our very bodies as a means of laying our case before the conscience of the local and national community. We were not unmindful of the difficulties involved. So we decided to go through a process of self-purification. We started having workshops on nonviolence and repeatedly asked ourselves the questions, "Are you able to accept blows without retaliating?" "Are you able to endure the ordeals of jail?"

15 We decided to set our direct action program around the Easter season, realizing that with the exception of Christmas, this was the largest shopping period of the year. Knowing that a strong economic withdrawal program would be the by-product of direct action, we felt that this was the best time to bring pressure on the merchants for the needed changes. Then it occurred to us that the March election was ahead, and so we speedily decided to postpone action until after election day. When we discovered that Mr. Connor was in the run-off, we decided again to postpone so that the demonstrations could not be used to cloud the issues. At this time we agreed to begin our nonviolent witness the day after the run-off.

This reveals that we did not move irresponsibly into direct action. We too wanted to see Mr. Connor defeated; so we went through postponement after postponement to aid in this community need. After this we felt that direct action could be delayed no longer.

You may well ask, "Why direct action? Why sit-ins, marches, etc.? Isn't negotiation a better path?" You are exactly right in your call for negotiation. Indeed, this is the purpose of direct action. Nonviolent direct action seeks to create such a crisis and establish such creative tension that a community that has constantly refused to negotiate is forced to confront the issue. It seeks so to dramatize the issue that it can no longer be ignored. I just referred to the creation of tension as a part of the work of the nonviolent resister. This may sound rather shocking. But I must confess that I am not afraid of the word tension. I have earnestly worked and preached against violent tension, but there is a type of constructive nonviolent tension that is necessary for growth. Just as Socrates felt that it was necessary to create a tension in the mind so that individuals could rise from the bondage of myths and half-truths to the unfettered realm of creative analysis and objective appraisal, we must see the need of having nonviolent gadflies to create the kind of tension in society that will help men rise from the dark depths of prejudice and racism to the majestic heights of understanding and brotherhood. So the purpose of the direct action is to create a situation so crisis-packed that it will inevitably open the door to negotiation. We, therefore, concur with you in your call for negotiation. Too long has our beloved Southland been bogged down in the tragic attempt to live in monologue rather than dialogue.

One of the basic points in your statement is that our acts are untimely. Some have asked, "Why didn't you give the new administration time to act?" The only answer that I can give to this inquiry is that the new administration must be prodded about as much as the outgoing one before it acts. We will be sadly mistaken if we feel that the election of Mr. Boutwell will bring the millennium to Birmingham. While Mr. Boutwell is much more articulate and gentle than Mr. Connor, they are both segregationists dedicated to the task of maintaining the status quo. The hope I see in Mr. Boutwell is that he will be reasonable enough to see the futility of massive resistance to desegregation. But he will not see this without pressure from the devotees of civil rights. My friends, I must say to you that we have not made a single gain in civil rights without determined legal and nonviolent pressure. History is the long and tragic story of the fact that privileged groups seldom give up their privileges voluntarily. Individuals may see the moral light and voluntarily give up their unjust posture; but as Reinhold Niebuhr has reminded us, groups are more immoral than individuals.

We know through painful experience that freedom is never voluntarily given by the oppressor; it must be demanded by the oppressed. Frankly I have never yet engaged in a direct action movement that was "well timed," according to the timetable of those who have not suffered unduly from the disease of segregation. For years now I have heard the word "Wait!" It rings in the ear of every Negro with a piercing familiarity. This "wait" has almost always meant "never." It has been a tranquilizing thalidomide, relieving the emotional stress for a moment, only to give birth to an ill-formed infant of frustration. We must come to see with the distinguished jurist of yesterday that "justice too long delayed is justice denied." We have waited for more than three hundred and forty years for our constitutional and God-given rights. The nations of Asia and Africa are moving with jet-like speed toward the goal of political independence, and we still creep at horse and buggy pace toward the gaining of a cup of coffee at a lunch counter.

20   I guess it is easy for those who have never felt the stinging darts 20 of segregation to say wait. But when you have seen vicious mobs lynch your mothers and fathers at will and drown your sisters and brothers at whim; when you have seen hate filled policemen curse, kick, brutalize, and even kill your black brothers and sisters with impunity; when you see the vast majority of your twenty million Negro brothers smothering in an air-tight cage of poverty in the midst of an affluent society; when you suddenly find your tongue twisted and your speech stammering as you seek to explain to your six-year-old daughter why she can't go to the public amusement park that has just been advertised on television, and see tears welling up in her little eyes when she is told that Funtown is closed to colored children, and see the depressing clouds of inferiority begin to form in her little mental sky, and see her begin to distort her little personality by unconsciously developing a bitterness toward white people; when you have to concoct an answer for a five-year-old son asking in agonizing pathos: "Daddy, why do white people treat colored people so mean?"; when you take a cross country drive and find it necessary to sleep night after night in the uncomfortable corners of your automobile because no motel will accept you; when you are humiliated day in and day out by nagging signs reading "white" and "colored"; when your first name becomes "nigger" and your middle name becomes "boy" (however old you are) and your last name becomes "John," and when your wife and mother are never given the respected title "Mrs."; when you are harried by day and haunted by night by the fact that you are a Negro, living constantly at tip-toe stance never quite knowing what to expect next, and plagued with inner fears and outer resentments; when you are forever

fighting a degenerating sense of "nobodiness";——then you will understand why we find it difficult to wait. There comes a time when the cup of endurance runs over, and men are no longer willing to be plunged into an abyss of injustice where they experience the bleakness of corroding despair. I hope, sirs, you can understand our legitimate and unavoidable impatience.

You express a great deal of anxiety over our willingness to break laws. This is certainly a legitimate concern. Since we so diligently urge people to obey the Supreme Court's decision of 1954 outlawing segregation in the public schools, it is rather strange and paradoxical to find us consciously breaking laws. One may well ask, "How can you advocate breaking some laws and obeying others?" The answer is found in the fact that there are two types of laws. There are *just* laws and there are *unjust* laws. I would be the first to advocate obeying just laws. One has not only a legal but moral responsibility to obey just laws. Conversely, one has a moral responsibility to disobey unjust laws. I would agree with Saint Augustine that "An unjust law is no law at all."

Now what is the difference between the two? How does one determine when a law is just or unjust? A just law is a man-made code that squares with the moral law or the law of God. An unjust law is a code that is out of harmony with the moral law. To put it in the terms of Saint Thomas Aquinas, an unjust law is a human law that is not rooted in eternal and natural law. Any law that uplifts human personality is just. Any law that degrades human personality is unjust. All segregation statutes are unjust because segregation distorts the soul and damages the personality. It gives the segregator a false sense of superiority and the segregated a false sense of inferiority. To use the words of Martin Buber, the great Jewish philosopher, segregation substitutes an "I-it" relationship for the "I-thou" relationship, and ends up relegating persons to the status of things. So segregation is not only politically, economically, and sociologically unsound, but it is morally wrong and sinful. Paul Tillich has said that sin is separation. Isn't segregation an existential expression of man's tragic separation, an expression of his awful estrangement, his terrible sinfulness? So I can urge men to obey the 1954 decision of the Supreme Court because it is morally right, and I can urge them to disobey segregation ordinances because they are morally wrong.

Let us turn to a more concrete example of just and unjust laws. An unjust law is a code that a majority inflicts on a minority that is not binding on itself. This is *difference* made legal. On the other hand a just law is a code that a majority compels a minority to follow that it is willing to follow itself. This is *sameness* made legal.

Let me give another explanation. An unjust law is a code inflicted upon a minority which that minority had no part in enacting or creating because they did not have the unhampered right to vote. Who can say the legislature of Alabama which set up the segregation laws was democratically elected? Throughout the state of Alabama all types of conniving methods are used to prevent Negroes from becoming registered voters and there are some counties without a single Negro registered to vote despite the fact that the Negro constitutes a majority of the population. Can any law set up in such a state be considered democratically structured?

25   These are just a few examples of unjust and just laws. There are 25 some instances when a law is just on its face but unjust in its application. For instance, I was arrested Friday on a charge of parading without a permit. Now there is nothing wrong with an ordinance which requires a permit for a parade, but when the ordinance is used to preserve segregation and to deny citizens the First Amendment privilege of peaceful assembly and peaceful protest, then it becomes unjust.

I hope you can see the distinction I am trying to point out. In no sense do I advocate evading or defying the law as the rabid segregationist would do. This would lead to anarchy. One who breaks an unjust law must do it *openly, lovingly* (not hatefully as the white mothers did in New Orleans when they were seen on television screaming "nigger, nigger, nigger") and with a willingness to accept the penalty. I submit that an individual who breaks a law that conscience tells him is unjust, and willingly accepts the penalty by staying in jail to arouse the conscience of the community over its injustice, is in reality expressing the very highest respect for law.

Of course there is nothing new about this kind of civil disobedience. It was seen sublimely in the refusal of Shadrach, Meshach, and Abednego to obey the laws of Nebuchadnezzar because a higher moral law was involved. It was practiced superbly by the early Christians who were willing to face hungry lions and the excruciating pain of chopping blocks, before submitting to certain unjust laws of the Roman Empire. To a degree academic freedom is a reality today because Socrates practiced civil disobedience.

We can never forget that everything Hitler did in Germany was "legal" and everything the Hungarian freedom fighters did in Hungary was "illegal." It was "illegal" to aid and comfort a Jew in Hitler's Germany. But I am sure that, if I had lived in Germany during that time, I would have aided and comforted my Jewish brothers even though it was illegal. If I lived in a communist country today where certain principles dear to the Christian faith are suppressed, I believe I would openly advocate disobeying those antireligious laws.

I must make two honest confessions to you, my Christian and Jewish brothers. First I must confess that over the last few years I have been gravely disappointed with the white moderate. I have almost reached the regrettable conclusion that the Negroes' great stumbling block in the stride toward freedom is not the White Citizens' "Counciler" or the Ku Klux Klanner, but the white moderate who is more devoted to "order" than to justice; who prefers a negative peace which is the absence of tension to a positive peace which is the presence of justice; who constantly says "I agree with you in the goal you seek, but I can't agree with your methods of direct action;" who paternalistically feels that he can set the timetable for another man's freedom; who lives by the myth of time and who constantly advises the Negro to wait until a "more convenient season." Shallow understanding from people of good will is more frustrating than absolute misunderstanding from people of ill will. Lukewarm acceptance is much more bewildering than outright rejection.

30   I had hoped that the white moderate would understand that law   30 and order exist for the purpose of establishing justice, and that when they fail to do this they become the dangerously structured dams that block the flow of social progress. I had hoped that the white moderate would understand that the present tension in the South is merely a necessary phase of the transition from an obnoxious negative peace, where the Negro passively accepted his unjust plight, to a substance-filled positive peace, where all men will respect the dignity and worth of human personality. Actually, we who engage in nonviolent direct action are not the creators of tension. We merely bring to the surface the hidden tension that is already alive. We bring it out in the open where it can be seen and dealt with. Like a boil that can never be cured as long as it is covered up but must be opened with all its pus-flowing ugliness to the natural medicines of air and light, injustice must likewise be exposed, with all of the tension its exposing creates, to the light

of human conscience and the air of national opinion before it can be cured.

In your statement you asserted that our actions, even though peaceful, must be condemned because they precipitate violence. But can this assertion be logically made? Isn't this like condemning the robbed man because his possession of money precipitated the evil act of robbery? Isn't this like condemning Socrates because his unswerving commitment to truth and his philosophical delvings precipitated the misguided popular mind to make him drink the hemlock? Isn't this like condemning Jesus because His unique God consciousness and never-ceasing devotion to His will precipitated the evil act of crucifixion? We must come to see, as federal courts have consistently affirmed, that it is immoral to urge an individual to withdraw his efforts to gain his basic constitutional rights because the quest precipitates violence. Society must protect the robbed and punish the robber.

I had also hoped that the white moderate would reject the myth of time. I received a letter this morning from a white brother in Texas which said: "All Christians know that the colored people will receive equal rights eventually, but is it possible that you are in too great of a religious hurry? It has taken Christianity almost 2,000 years to accomplish what it has. The teachings of Christ take time to come to earth." All that is said here grows out of a tragic misconception of time. It is the strangely irrational notion that there is something in the very flow of time that will inevitably cure all ills. Actually time is neutral. It can be used either destructively or constructively. I am coming to feel that the people of ill will have used time much more effectively than the people of good will. We will have to repent in this generation not merely for the vitriolic words and actions of the bad people, but for the appalling silence of the good people. We must come to see that human progress never rolls in on wheels of inevitability. It comes through the tireless efforts and persistent work of men willing to be co-workers with God, and without this hard work time itself becomes an ally of the forces of social stagnation.

We must use time creatively, and forever realize that the time is always ripe to do right. Now is the time to make real the promise of democracy, and transform our pending national elegy into a creative psalm of brotherhood. Now is the time to lift our national policy from the quicksand of racial injustice to the solid rock of human dignity.

You spoke of our activity in Birmingham as extreme. At first I was rather disappointed that fellow clergymen would see my nonviolent efforts as those of the extremist. I started thinking about the fact that I stand in the middle of two opposing forces in the Negro community. One is a force of complacency made up of Negroes who, as a result of long years of oppression, have been so completely drained of self-respect and a sense of "somebodiness" that they have adjusted to segregation, and of a few Negroes in the middle class who, because of a degree of academic and economic security, and because at points they profit by segregation, have unconsciously become insensitive to the problems of the masses. The other force is one of bitterness and hatred and comes perilously close to advocating violence. It is expressed in the various black nationalist groups that are springing up over the nation, the largest and best known being Elijah Muhammad's Muslim movement. This movement is nourished by the contemporary frustration over the continued existence of racial discrimination. It is made up of people who have lost faith in America, who have absolutely repudiated Christianity, and who have concluded that the white man is an incurable "devil." I have tried to stand between these two forces saying that we need not follow the "do-nothingism" of the complacent or the hatred and despair of the black nationalist. There is the more excellent way of love and nonviolent protest. I'm grateful to God that, through the Negro church, the dimension of nonviolence entered our struggle. If this philosophy had not emerged I am convinced that by now many streets of the South would be flowing with floods of blood. And I am further convinced that if our white brothers dismiss us as "rabble rousers" and "outside agitators"—those of us who are working through the channels of nonviolent direct action—and refuse to support our nonviolent efforts, millions of Negroes, out of frustration and despair, will seek solace and security in black nationalist ideologies, a development that will lead inevitably to a frightening racial nightmare.

35   Oppressed people cannot remain oppressed forever. The urge for 35 freedom will eventually come. This is what has happened to the American Negro. Something within has reminded him of his birthright of freedom; something without has reminded him that he can gain it. Consciously and unconsciously, he has been swept in by what the Germans call the *Zeitgeist*, and with his black brothers of Africa, and his brown and yellow brothers of Asia, South America, and the

Caribbean, he is moving with a sense of cosmic urgency toward the promised land of racial justice. Recognizing this vital urge that has engulfed the Negro community, one should readily understand public demonstrations. The Negro has many pent-up resentments and latent frustrations. He has to get them out. So let him march sometime; let him have his prayer pilgrimages to the city hall; understand why he must have sit-ins and freedom rides. If his repressed emotions do not come out in these nonviolent ways, they will come out in ominous expressions of violence. This is not a threat; it is a fact of history. So I have not said to my people, "Get rid of your discontent." But I have tried to say that this normal and healthy discontent can be channeled through the creative outlet of nonviolent direct action. Now this approach is being dismissed as extremist. I must admit that I was initially disappointed in being so categorized.

But as I continued to think about the matter I gradually gained a bit of satisfaction from being considered an extremist. Was not Jesus an extremist in love? "Love your enemies, bless them that curse you, pray for them that despitefully use you." Was not Amos an extremist for justice— "Let justice roll down like waters and righteousness like a mighty stream." Was not Paul an extremist for the gospel of Jesus Christ— "I bear in my body the marks of the Lord Jesus." Was not Martin Luther an extremist— "Here I stand; I can do none other so help me God." Was not John Bunyan an extremist— "I will stay in jail to the end of my days before I make a butchery of my conscience." Was not Abraham Lincoln an extremist— "This nation cannot survive half slave and half free." Was not Thomas Jefferson an extremist— "We hold these truths to be self evident that all men are created equal." So the question is not whether we will be extremist but what kind of extremist will we be. Will we be extremists for hate or will we be extremists for love? Will we be extremists for the preservation of injustice or will we be extremists for the cause of justice? In that dramatic scene on Calvary's hill three men were crucified. We must never forget that all three were crucified for the same crime—the crime of extremism. Two were extremists for immorality, and thus fell below their environment. The other, Jesus Christ, was an extremist for love, truth, and goodness, and thereby rose above His environment. So, after all, maybe the South, the nation, and the world are in dire need of creative extremists.

I had hoped that the white moderate would see this. Maybe I was too optimistic. Maybe I expected too much. I guess I should have realized that few members of a race that has oppressed another race can understand or appreciate the deep groans and passionate yearnings of those that have been oppressed, and still fewer have the vision to see that injustice must be rooted out by strong, persistent, and determined action. I am thankful, however, that some of our white brothers have grasped the meaning of this social revolution and committed themselves to it. They are still all too small in quantity, but they are big in quality. Some like Ralph McGill, Lillian Smith, Harry Golden, and James Dabbs have written about our struggle in eloquent, prophetic, and understanding terms. Others have marched with us down nameless streets of the South. They have languished in filthy, roach-infested jails, suffering the abuse and brutality of angry policemen who see them as "dirty nigger lovers." They, unlike so many of their moderate brothers and sisters, have recognized the urgency of the moment and sensed the need for powerful "action" antidotes to combat the disease of segregation.

Let me rush on to mention my other disappointment. I have been so greatly disappointed with the white Church and its leadership. Of course there are some notable exceptions. I am not unmindful of the fact that each of you has taken some significant stands on this issue. I commend you, Rev. Stallings, for your Christian stand on this past Sunday, in welcoming Negroes to your worship service on a nonsegregated basis. I commend the Catholic leaders of this state for integrating Springhill College several years ago.

But despite these notable exceptions I must honestly reiterate that I have been disappointed with the Church. I do not say that as one of those negative critics who can always find something wrong with the Church. I say it as a minister of the gospel, who loves the Church; who was nurtured in its bosom; who has been sustained by its spiritual blessings and who will remain true to it as long as the cord of life shall lengthen.

40   I had the strange feeling when I was suddenly catapulted into the   40
leadership of the bus protest in Montgomery several years ago that we would have the support of the white Church. I felt that the white ministers, priests, and rabbis of the South would be some of our strongest allies. Instead, some have been outright opponents, refusing to understand the

freedom movement and misrepresenting its leaders; all too many others have been more cautious than courageous and have remained silent behind the anesthetizing security of stained glass windows.

In spite of my shattered dreams of the past, I came to Birmingham with the hope that the white religious leadership of the community would see the justice of our cause and, with deep moral concern, serve as the channel through which our just grievances could get to the power structure. I had hoped that each of you would understand. But again I have been disappointed.

I have heard numerous religious leaders of the South call upon their worshippers to comply with a desegregation decision because it is the law, but I have longed to hear white ministers say follow this decree because integration is morally right and the Negro is your brother. In the midst of blatant injustices inflicted upon the Negro, I have watched white churches stand on the sideline and merely mouth pious irrelevancies and sanctimonious trivialities. In the midst of a mighty struggle to rid our nation of racial and economic injustice, I have heard so many ministers say, "Those are social issues with which the Gospel has no real concern," and I have watched so many churches commit themselves to a completely otherworldly religion which made a strange distinction between body and soul, the sacred and the secular.

So here we are moving toward the exit of the twentieth century with a religious community largely adjusted to the status quo, standing as a tail light behind other community agencies rather than a headlight leading men to higher levels of justice.

I have travelled the length and breadth of Alabama, Mississippi, and all the other Southern states. On sweltering summer days and crisp autumn mornings I have looked at her beautiful churches with their spires pointing heavenward. I have beheld the impressive outlay of her massive religious education buildings. Over and over again I have found myself asking: "Who worships here? Who is their God? Where were their voices when the lips of Governor Barnett dripped with words of interposition and nullification? Where were they when Governor Wallace gave the clarion call for defiance and hatred? Where were their voices of support when tired, bruised, and weary Negro men and women decided to rise from the dark dungeons of complacency to the bright hills of creative protest?"

45 Yes, these questions are still in my mind. In deep disappointment, 45
I have wept over the laxity of the Church. But be assured that my tears

have been tears of love. There can be no deep disappointment where there is not deep love. Yes, I love the Church; I love her sacred walls. How could I do otherwise? I am in the rather unique position of being the son, the grandson, and the great grandson of preachers. Yes, I see the Church as the body of Christ. But, oh! How we have blemished and scarred that body through social neglect and fear of being non-conformists.

There was a time when the Church was very powerful. It was during that period when the early Christians rejoiced when they were deemed worthy to suffer for what they believed. In those days the Church was not merely a thermometer that recorded the ideas and principles of popular opinion; it was a thermostat that transformed the mores of society. Wherever the early Christians entered a town the power structure got disturbed and immediately sought to convict them for being "disturbers of the peace" and "outside agitators." But they went on with the conviction that they were a "colony of heaven" and had to obey God rather than man. They were small in number but big in commitment. They were too God-intoxicated to be "astronomically intimidated." They brought an end to such ancient evils as infanticide and gladiatorial contest.

Things are different now. The contemporary Church is so often a weak, ineffectual voice with an uncertain sound. It is so often the arch-supporter of the status quo. Far from being disturbed by the presence of the Church, the power structure of the average community is consoled by the Church's silent and often vocal sanction of things as they are.

But the judgment of God is upon the Church as never before. If the Church of today does not recapture the sacrificial spirit of the early Church, it will lose its authentic ring, forfeit the loyalty of millions, and be dismissed as an irrelevant social club with no meaning for the twentieth century. I am meeting young people every day whose disappointment with the Church has risen to outright disgust.

Maybe again I have been too optimistic. Is organized religion too inextricably bound to the status quo to save our nation and the world? Maybe I must turn my faith to the inner spiritual Church, the church within the Church, as the true *ecclesia* and the hope of the world. But again I am thankful to God that some noble souls from the ranks of organized religion have broken loose from the paralyzing chains of conformity and joined us as active partners in the struggle for freedom. They have left their secure congregations and walked the streets of Albany, Georgia, with us. They have gone through the highways of the South on torturous rides for freedom. Yes, they have gone to jail with us. Some have been kicked out of their churches and lost the support of their bishops and fellow ministers. But they have gone with the faith that right defeated is stronger than evil triumphant. These men have been the leaven in the lump of the race. Their witness has been the spiritual salt that has preserved the true meaning of the Gospel in these troubled times. They have carved a tunnel of hope through the dark mountain of disappointment.

50   I hope the Church as a whole will meet the challenge of this decisive hour. But even if the Church does not come to the aid of justice, I have no despair about the future. I have no fear about the outcome of our struggle in Birmingham, even if our motives are presently misunderstood. We will reach the goal of freedom in Birmingham and all over the nation, because the goal of America is freedom. Abused and scorned though we may be, our destiny is tied up with the destiny of America. Before the pilgrims landed at Plymouth, we were here. Before the pen of Jefferson etched across the pages of history the majestic words of the Declaration of Independence, we were here. For more than two centuries our foreparents labored in this country without wages; they made cotton "king"; and they built the homes of their masters in the midst of brutal injustice and shameful humiliation—and yet out of a bottomless vitality they continued to thrive and develop. If the inexpressible cruelties of slavery could not stop us, the opposition we now face will surely fail. We will win our freedom because the sacred heritage of our nation and the eternal will of God are embodied in our echoing demands.   50

I must close now. But before closing I am impelled to mention one other point in your statement that troubled me profoundly. You warmly commended the Birmingham police force for keeping "order" and "preventing violence." I don't believe you would have so warmly commended the police force if you had seen its angry violent dogs literally biting six unarmed, nonviolent Negroes. I don't believe you would so quickly commend the policemen if you would observe their ugly and inhuman treatment of Negroes here in the city jail; if you would watch them push and curse old Negro women and young Negro girls; if you would see them slap and kick old Negro men and young Negro boys; if you will observe them, as they did on two occasions, refuse to give us food because we wanted to sing our grace together. I'm sorry that I can't join you in your praise for the police department.

It is true that they have been rather disciplined in their public handling of the demonstrators. In this sense they have been rather publicly "nonviolent." But for what purpose? To preserve the evil system of segregation. Over the last few years I have consistently preached that nonviolence demands that the means we use must be as pure as the ends we seek. So I have tried to make it clear that it is wrong to use immoral means to attain moral ends. But now I must affirm that it is just as wrong, or even more so, to use moral means to preserve immoral ends. Maybe Mr. Connor and his policemen have been rather publicly nonviolent, as Chief Pritchett was in Albany, Georgia, but they have used the moral means of nonviolence to maintain the immoral end of flagrant racial injustice. T. S. Eliot has said that there is no greater treason than to do the right deed for the wrong reason.

I wish you had commended the Negro sit-inners and demonstrators of Birmingham for their sublime courage, their willingness to suffer, and their amazing discipline in the midst of the most inhuman provocation. One day the South will recognize its real heroes. They will be the James Merediths, courageously and with a majestic sense of purpose, facing jeering and hostile mobs and the agonizing loneliness that characterizes the life of the pioneer. They will be old, oppressed, battered Negro women, symbolized in a seventy-two year old woman of Montgomery, Alabama, who rose up with a sense of dignity and with her people decided not to ride the segregated buses, and responded to one who inquired about her tiredness with ungrammatical profundity: "My feets is tired, but my soul is rested." They will be young high school and college students, young ministers of the gospel and a host of the elders, courageously and nonviolently sitting in at lunch counters and willingly going to jail for conscience sake. One day the South will know that when these disinherited children of God sat down at lunch counters they were in reality standing up for the best in the American dream and the most sacred values in our Judeo-Christian heritage, and thus carrying our whole nation back to great wells of democracy which were dug deep by the founding fathers in the formulation of the Constitution and the Declaration of Independence.

Never before have I written a letter this long (or should I say a book?). I'm afraid that it is much too long to take your precious time.

I can assure you that it would have been much shorter if I had been writing from a comfortable desk, but what else is there to do when you are alone for days in the dull monotony of a narrow jail cell other than write long letters, think strange thoughts, and pray long prayers!

55   If I have said anything in this letter that is an overstatement of the truth and is indicative of an unreasonable impatience, I beg you to forgive me. If I have said anything in this letter that is an understatement of the truth and is indicative of my having a patience that makes me patient with anything less than brotherhood, I beg God to forgive me.

I hope this letter finds you strong in the faith. I also hope that circumstances will soon make it possible for me to meet each of you, not as an integrationist or a civil rights leader, but as a fellow clergyman and a Christian brother. Let us all hope that the dark clouds of racial prejudice will soon pass away and the deep fog of misunderstanding will be lifted from our fear-drenched communities and in some not too distant tomorrow the radiant stars of love and brotherhood will shine over our great nation with all of their scintillating beauty.

Yours for the cause of
Peace and Brotherhood
MARTIN LUTHER KING, JR.

Questions on Meaning

1. At the time that this essay was written, King had been active in the civil rights movement for nearly 10 years. How had he usually handled criticisms of his work and ideas? Why?
2. The public statement by the eight clergymen exhibits a distrust for *outsiders*. How does King address that common fear and skepticism? If you had been one of the *local* clergymen, how do you think you would have reacted to King's explanation? Would you have respected his convictions? Embraced his beliefs?
3. Often in this essay, King addresses the issue of the timeliness of nonviolent demonstrations and other political activities. This urgency of action is a common theme of King's. "For years I have heard the word 'Wait!' " he writes. "It rings in the ear of every Negro with a piercing familiarity." What does the word *wait* mean to King?

Questions on Rhetorical Strategy and Style

1. King's dominant rhetorical strategy is clear: persuasion. He is not telling a story; he is not using flowery language or a preacher's oratory. This essay is logos and ethos: a sound argument supported by credibility, integrity, and experience. Analyze how he builds the argument one step at a time through the essay.
2. Repetition helps to drive home an argument. Show two places in this essay where King effectively uses repetition. Rewrite one of the passages without the repeated phrase and compare its effectiveness with the original.
3. Find King's discussion of just and unjust laws and locate the two paragraphs in which he gives examples of these laws ("Let us turn to a more concrete example . . . " and "Let me give another explanation . . . "). What is your reaction to his use of examples here?

Writing Assignments

1. A student of Gandhi, King based his political activities on nonviolent confrontation. In this essay, King outlines four steps of nonviolent activism: collect facts, negotiate, self-purify, and take direct action. Identify an injustice in your lifetime that people are trying or have tried to change through nonviolent activism.

Examples may include a physical barrier to people with physical handicaps, an employment restriction that discriminates against elderly people, or a city ordinance that unfairly restricts the activities of teenagers. Describe the political activity that has occurred, then relate it to King's four steps. Were these steps applied? If not, discuss how the outcome might have been different if these steps had been applied.

2. In this essay, King responds to the charge of being an extremist by admitting that he initially was put off by the label, but then realized that he wore it proudly. What is your reaction to the term? Does "extremist" hold negative or positive connotations for you? Is it used to credit or discredit? Identify some current political figures who are called extremists. Write an essay defining the term and describing how it is commonly applied, using current extremist political figures as examples.

3. King writes that one "has a moral responsibility to disobey unjust laws." Do you agree? Reread his defense of that statement. Does King's stance help overturn unjust laws or create anarchy? Choose a "law" that affects your life that you feel is unjust—perhaps a dormitory rule or campus restriction or a local law. Would you, or do you, intentionally break it? Write an essay describing the "law" and your action, arguing your viewpoint on obeying or disobeying it.

A Modest Proposal

Jonathan Swift

*Born in Dublin, Ireland, Jonathan Swift (1667–1745)
entered the clergy after his education at Trinity College and
Oxford University. Through his long life he wrote in a wide
range of genres, including poetry, religious pamphlets, essays, and satires on various social and political themes. His
best-known work is* Gulliver's Travels, *a combination of
children's story and social satire. Swift was always a sup-
porter of Irish causes, as can be seen in "A Modest Proposal," which was published anonymously in 1729. In this
ironic essay, the speaker—the "I"—is not Swift himself but
a persona, a fictional voice who gives his proposal to cure
the ills of contemporary Ireland. It is true that Ireland at
this time had the problems described by this persona:
poverty, unemployment, a failing economy, exploitation by
the wealthy classes, conflict between the Anglican and
Catholic churches, and so on. This is the serious subject
Swift addresses through his satire. If you have not read or
heard of his "proposal" previously, read slowly and atten-
tively: you might be greatly surprised to learn the nature of
his proposition.*

1   It is a melancholy object to those who walk through this great town   1
or travel in the country, when they see the streets, the roads, and
cabin doors, crowded with beggars of the female sex, followed by
three, four, or six children, all in rags and importuning every passen-
ger for an alms. These mothers, instead of being able to work for their
honest livelihood, are forced to employ all their time in strolling to
beg sustenance for their helpless infants, who, as they grow up, either
turn thieves for want of work, or leave their dear native country to
fight for the Pretender in Spain, or sell themselves to the Barbadoes.

I think it is agreed by all parties that this prodigious number of
children in the arms, or on the backs, or at the heels of their mothers,

and frequently of their fathers, is in the present deplorable state of the kingdom a very great additional grievance; and therefore whoever could find out a fair, cheap, and easy method of making these children sound, useful members of the commonwealth would deserve so well of the public as to have his statue set up for a preserver of the nation.

But my intention is very far from being confined to provide only for the children of professed beggars; it is of a much greater extent, and shall take in the whole number of infants at a certain age who are born of parents in effect as little able to support them as those who demand our charity in the streets.

As to my own part, having turned my thoughts for many years upon this important subject, and maturely weighed the several schemes of other projectors, I have always found them grossly mistaken in their computation. It is true, a child just dropped from its dam may be supported by her milk for a solar year, with little other nourishment; at most not above the value of two shillings, which the mother may certainly get, or the value in scraps, by her lawful occupation of begging; and it is exactly at one year old that I propose to provide for them in such a manner as instead of being a charge upon their parents or the parish, or wanting food and raiment for the rest of their lives, they shall on the contrary contribute to the feeding, and partly to the clothing, of many thousands.

5   There is likewise another great advantage in my scheme, that it   5 will prevent those voluntary abortions, and that horrid practice of women murdering their bastard children, alas, too frequent among us, sacrificing the poor innocent babes, I doubt, more to avoid the expense than the shame, which would move tears and pity in the most savage and inhuman breast.

The number of souls in this kingdom being usually reckoned one million and a half, of these I calculate there may be about two hundred thousand couples whose wives are breeders; from which number I subtract thirty thousand couples who are able to maintain their own children, although I apprehend there cannot be so many under the present distresses of the kingdom; but this being granted, there will remain an hundred and seventy thousand breeders. I again subtract fifty thousand for those women who miscarry, or whose children die by accident or disease within the year. There only remain an hundred and twenty thousand children of poor parents annually born. The question therefore is, how this number shall be reared and provided for, which, as I have already said, under the present situation of affairs, is utterly impossible by all the methods hitherto proposed. For we can neither employ them in handicraft nor agriculture; we neither build houses (I mean in the country) nor cultivate land. They can very seldom pick up livelihood by stealing till they arrive at six years old, except where they are of towardly parts; although I confess they learn the rudiments much earlier, during which time they can however be looked upon only as probationers, as I have been informed by a principal gentleman in the county of Cavan, who protested to me that he never knew above one or two instances under the age of six, even in a part of the kingdom so renowned for the quickest proficiency in that art.

I am assured by our merchants that a boy or a girl before twelve years old is no salable commodity; and even when they come to this age, they will not yield above three pounds, or three pounds and half a crown at most on the Exchange; which cannot turn to account either to the parents or the kingdom, the charge of nutriment and rags having been at least four times that value.

I shall now therefore humbly propose my own thoughts, which I hope will not be liable to the least objection.

I have been assured by a very knowing American of my acquaintance in London, that a young healthy child well nursed is at a year old a most delicious, nourishing, and wholesome food, whether stewed, roasted, baked, or boiled; and I make no doubt that it will equally serve in a fricassee or a ragout.

10   I do therefore humbly offer it to public consideration that of the   10 hundred and twenty thousand children, already computed, twenty thousand may be reserved for breed, whereof only one fourth part to be males, which is more than we allow to sheep, black cattle, or swine; and my reason is that these children are seldom the fruits of marriage, a circumstance not much regarded by our savages, therefore one male will be sufficient to serve four females. That the remaining hundred thousand may at a year old be offered in sale to the persons of quality and fortune through the kingdom, always advising the mother to let them suck plentifully in the last month, so as to render them plump and fat for a good table. A child will make two dishes at an entertainment for friends; and when the family dines alone, the fore or hind quarter will make a reasonable dish, and seasoned with a little pepper or salt will be very good boiled on the fourth day, especially in winter.

I have reckoned upon a medium that a child just born will weigh twelve pounds, and in a solar year if tolerably nursed increaseth to twenty-eight pounds.

I grant this food will be somewhat dear, and therefore very proper for landlords, who, as they have already devoured most of the parents, seem to have the best title to the children.

Infant's flesh will be in season throughout the year, but more plentiful in March, and a little before and after. For we are told by a grave author, an eminent French physician, that fish being a prolific diet, there are more children born in Roman Catholic countries about nine months after Lent, than at any other season; therefore, reckoning a year after Lent, the markets will be more glutted than usual, because the number of popish infants is at least three to one in this kingdom; and therefore it will have one other collateral advantage, by lessening the number of Papists among us.

I have already computed the charge of nursing a beggar's child (in which list I reckon all cottagers, laborers, and four fifths of the farmers) to be about two shillings per annum, rags included; and I believe no gentleman would repine to give ten shillings for the carcass of a good fat child, which, as I have said, will make four dishes of excellent nutritive meat, when he hath only some particular friend or his own family to dine with him. Thus the squire will learn to be a good landlord, and grow popular among the tenants; the mother will have eight shillings net profit, and be fit for work till she produces another child.

15 Those who are more thrifty (as I must confess the times require) 15 may flay the carcass; the skin of which artificially dressed will make admirable gloves for ladies, and summer boots for fine gentlemen.

As to our city of Dublin, shambles may be appointed for this purpose in the most convenient parts of it, and butchers we may be assured will not be wanting; although I rather recommend buying the children alive, and dressing them hot from the knife as we do roasting pigs.

A very worthy person, a true lover of his country, and whose virtues I highly esteem, was lately pleased in discoursing on this matter to offer a refinement upon my scheme. He said that many gentlemen of his kingdom, having of late destroyed their deer, he conceived that the want of venison might be well supplied by the bodies of young lads and maidens, not exceeding fourteen years of age nor under twelve, so great a number of both sexes in every county being now ready to starve for want of work and service; and these to be disposed of by their parents, if alive, or otherwise by their nearest relations. But with due deference to so excellent a friend and so deserving a patriot, I cannot be altogether in his sentiments; for as to the males, my American acquaintance assured me from frequent experience that their flesh was generally tough and lean, like that of our schoolboys, by continual exercise, and their taste disagreeable; and to fatten them would not answer the charge. Then as to the females, it would, I think with humble submission, be a loss to the public, because they soon would become breeders themselves; and besides, it is not improbable that some scrupulous people might be apt to censure such a practice (although indeed very unjustly) as a little bordering upon cruelty; which, I confess, hath always been with me the strongest objection against any project, how well soever intended.

But in order to justify my friend, he confessed that this expedient was put into his head by the famous Psalmanazar, a native of the island Formosa, who came from thence to London above twenty years ago, and in conversation told my friend that in his country when any young person happened to be put to death, the executioner sold the carcass to persons of quality as a prime dainty; and that in his time the body of a plump girl of fifteen, who was crucified for an attempt to poison the emperor, was sold to his Imperial Majesty's prime minister of state, and other great mandarins of the court, in joints from the gibbet, at four hundred crowns. Neither indeed can I deny that if the same use were made of several plump young girls in this town, who without one single groat to their fortunes cannot stir abroad without a chair, and appear at the playhouse and assemblies in foreign fineries which they never will pay for, the kingdom would not be the worse.

Some persons of a desponding spirit are in great concern about that vast number of poor people who are aged, diseased, or maimed, and I have been desired to employ my thoughts what course may be taken to ease the nation of so grievous an encumbrance. But I am not in the least pain upon that matter, because it is very well known that they are every day dying and rotting by cold and famine, and filth and vermin, as fast as can be reasonably expected. And as to the younger laborers, they are now in almost as hopeful a condition. They cannot get work, and consequently pine away for want of nourishment to a degree that if any time they are accidentally hired to common labor, they have not strength to perform it; and thus the country and themselves are happily delivered from the evils to come.

20   I have too long digressed, and therefore shall return to my subject. I think the advantages by the proposal which I have made are obvious and many, as well as of the highest importance.   20

For first, as I have already observed, it would greatly lessen the number of Papists, with whom we are yearly overrun, being the principal breeders of the nation as well as our most dangerous enemies; and who stay at home on purpose to deliver the kingdom to the Pretender, hoping to take their advantage by the absence of so many good Protestants, who have chosen rather to leave their country than to stay at home and pay tithes against their conscience to an Episcopal curate.

Secondly, the poorer tenants will have something valuable of their own, which by law may be made liable to distress, and help to pay their landlord's rent, their corn and cattle being already seized and money a thing unknown.

Thirdly, whereas the maintenance of an hundred thousand children, from two years old and upwards, cannot be computed at less than ten shillings a piece per annum, the nation's stock will be thereby increased fifty thousand pounds per annum, besides the profit of a new dish introduced to the tables of all gentlemen of fortune in the kingdom who have any refinement in taste. And the money will circulate among ourselves, the goods being entirely of our own growth and manufacture.

Fourthly, the constant breeders, besides the gain of eight shillings sterling per annum by the sale of their children, will be rid of the charge of maintaining them after the first year.

25   Fifthly, this food would likewise bring great custom to taverns,   25 where the vintners will certainly be so prudent as to procure the best receipts for dressing it to perfection, and consequently have their houses frequented by all the fine gentlemen, who justly value themselves upon their knowledge in good eating; and a skillful cook, who understands how to oblige his guests, will contrive to make it as expensive as they please.

Sixthly, this would be a great inducement to marriage, which all wise nations have either encouraged by rewards or enforced by laws and penalties. It would increase the care and tenderness of mothers toward their children, when they were sure of a settlement for life to the poor babes, provided in some sort by the public, to their annual profit instead of expense. We should see an honest emulation among the married women, which of them could bring the fattest child to the market. Men would become as fond of their wives during the time of pregnancy as they are now of their mares in foal, their cows in calf, or sows when they are ready to farrow; nor offer to beat or kick them (as is too frequent a practice) for fear of a miscarriage.

Many other advantages might be enumerated. For instance, the addition of some thousand carcasses in our exportation of barreled beef, the propagation of swine's flesh, and improvement in the art of making good bacon, so much wanted among us by the great destruction of pigs, too frequent at our tables, which are no way comparable in taste or magnificence to a well-grown, fat, yearling child, which roasted whole will make a considerable figure at a lord mayor's feast or any other public entertainment. But this and many others I omit, being studious of brevity.

Supposing that one thousand families in this city would be constant customers for infants' flesh, besides others who might have it at merry meetings, particularly weddings and christenings, I compute that Dublin would take off annually about twenty thousand carcasses, and the rest of the kingdom (where probably they will be sold somewhat cheaper) the remaining eighty thousand.

I can think of no one objection that will possibly be raised against this proposal, unless it should be urged that the number of people will be thereby much lessened in the kingdom. This I freely own, and it was indeed one principal design in offering it to the world. I desire the reader will observe; that I calculate my remedy for this one individual kingdom of Ireland and for no other that ever was, is, or I think ever can be upon earth. Therefore, let no man talk to me of other expedients: of taxing our absentees at five shillings a pound: of using neither clothes nor household furniture except what is of our own growth and manufacture: of utterly rejecting the materials and instruments that promote foreign luxury: of curing the expensiveness of pride, vanity, idleness, and gaming in our women: of introducing a vein of parsimony, prudence, and temperance: of learning to love our country, in the want of which we differ even from Laplanders and the inhabitants of Topinamboo: of quitting our animosities and factions, nor acting any longer like the Jews, who were murdering one another at the very moment their city was taken: of being a little cautious not to sell our country and conscience for nothing: of teaching landlords to have at least one degree of mercy toward their tenants: lastly, of putting a spirit of honesty, industry, and skill into our shopkeepers; who, if a resolution could now be taken to buy only our native goods, would immediately unite to cheat and exact upon us in the price, the measure, and the goodness, nor could ever yet be brought to make one fair proposal of just dealing, though often and earnestly invited to it.

30   Therefore, I repeat, let no man talk to me of these and the like expedients, till he hath at least some glimpse of hope that there will ever be some hearty and sincere attempt to put them in practice.

But as to myself, having been wearied out for many years with offering vain, idle, visionary thoughts, and at length utterly despairing of success, I fortunately fell upon this proposal, which, as it is wholly new, so it hath something solid and real, of no expense and little trouble, full in our own power, and whereby we can incur no danger in disobliging England. For this kind of commodity will not bear exportation, the flesh being of too tender a consistence to admit a long continuance in salt, although perhaps I could name a country which would be glad to eat up our whole nation without it.

After all, I am not so violently bent upon my own opinion as to reject any offer proposed by wise men, which shall be found equally innocent, cheap, easy, and effectual. But before something of that kind shall be advanced in contradiction to my scheme, and offering a better, I desire the author or authors will be pleased maturely to consider two points. First, as things now stand, how they will be able to find food and raiment for an hundred thousand useless mouths and backs. And secondly, there being a round million of creatures in human figure throughout this kingdom, whose sole subsistence put into a common stock would leave them in debt two millions of pounds sterling, adding those who are beggars by profession to the bulk of farmers, cottagers, and laborers, with their wives and children who are beggars in effect; I desire those politicians who dislike my overture, and may perhaps be so bold to attempt an answer, that they will first ask the parents of these mortals whether they would not at this day think it a great happiness to have been sold for food at a year old in this manner I prescribe, and thereby have avoided such a perpetual scene of misfortunes as they have since gone through by the oppression of landlords, the impossibility of paying rent without money or trade, the want of common sustenance, with neither house nor clothes to cover them from the inclemencies of the weather, and the most inevitable prospect of entailing the like or greater miseries upon their breed forever.

I profess, in the sincerity of my heart, that I have not the least personal interest in endeavoring to promote this necessary work, having no other motive than the public good of my country, by advancing our trade, providing for infants, relieving the poor, and giving some pleasure to the rich. I have no children by which I can propose to get a single penny; the youngest being nine years old, and my wife past childbearing.

Questions on Meaning

1. Some readers, unfamiliar with satire and perhaps misled by a different use of the English language in another culture almost 300 years ago, read this essay through to the end thinking the author is seriously proposing eating human infants. Indeed, that perfectly serious tone is part of why this essay is so successful and is still read today, as Swift avoids "giving away" the joke by going too far in his exaggeration. Yet even a reader unfamiliar with satire should discern the many ways the essay shows Swift is sympathetic with the plight of the poverty-stricken people of whom he writes. Reread the essay and look for several examples of this sympathy.

2. Given the severity of the social problem Swift is reacting to, one might think he should have taken a more direct approach in addressing it. Why do you think Swift chose irony and what does this method add to the meaning of the essay?

Questions on Rhetorical Strategy and Style

1. At what point did you begin to realize the irony of the essay? Reread the first three paragraphs and underline words and phrases that begin to build the satire from the very beginning. How does Swift continue to build the satire gradually up to the proposal itself in paragraph 10?

2. In this form of irony, things are apt to be the opposite of what is said. In particular, the "fine gentlemen" and landlords mentioned throughout the essay are not actually being praised. Find as many references as you can in the essay to this ruling class, and consider how they, as cannibals, bear the true brunt of Swift's satire.

3. A prominent characteristic of Swift's style in this essay is his use of detail, such as the exact numbers of children and percentages for breeding, specific recipes and seasonings, and exact monetary values versus costs. What effect does this specificity contribute to the essay?

4. Find the paragraph near the end of the essay in which Swift reveals his serious suggestions for solving Ireland's problems. How can you tell these are serious, not ironic, proposals?

5. Swift in this essays uses persuasive rhetorical strategies, even though he turns them upside-down with his satire. A persuasive essay may typically describe a problem, offer a solution, explain the benefits of the solution, and argue the superiority of this solution

over others. Identify these strategies in Swift's essay and explain how he uses them.

Writing Assignments

1. The essay describes some elements of a society in which one class controls resources and exploits another. Have there been any parallels to this in America's history? Explain how some problems such as poverty relate to the presence of different socioeconomic classes.

2. Satire is a particular form of humor in which something can be condemned by praise, for example, or praised by condemnation. What other examples of satire can you identify in today's culture, including works of fiction, movies or television, and newspapers? Has the basic technique of ironic exaggeration changed?

Gender

Sex, Lies, and Conversation
Deborah Tannen

*Deborah Tannen (1945–), born in Brooklyn, New York,
received her Ph.D. in linguistics from the University of
California, Berkeley and teaches at Georgetown University.
Her research into how people communicate has brought her
critical and popular acclaim, and she has appeared on several television programs and has written for* The New
York Times, *the* Washington Post, *and* Vogue. *Her book*
That's Not What I Meant *(1987) analyzes the effects of
conversational styles on relationships.* You Just Don't Understand *(1990), in which the following selection was included, examines differences in how men and women
converse.* Talking From 9 to 5 *(1994) resulted from her
research into conversational styles in work settings and
their impact on how work is performed and who gets
ahead. The following essay, which first appeared in* The
New York Times, *is based on her scientific study of the
conversational patterns of men and women and how differences in these styles lead to misinterpretation, tension,
and sometimes divorce.*

1   I was addressing a small gathering in a suburban Virginia living   1
room—a women's group that had invited men to join them.
Throughout the evening, one man had been particularly talkative,
frequently offering ideas and anecdotes, while his wife sat silently beside him on the couch. Toward the end of the evening, I commented
that women frequently complain that their husbands don't talk to
them. This man quickly concurred. He gestured toward his wife and
said, "She's the talker in our family." The room burst into laughter;

the man looked puzzled and hurt. "It's true," he explained. "When I come home from work I have nothing to say. If she didn't keep the conversation going, we'd spend the whole evening in silence."

This episode crystallizes the irony that although American men tend to talk more than women in public situations, they often talk less at home. And this pattern is wreaking havoc with marriage.

The pattern was observed by political scientist Andrew Hacker in the late '70s. Sociologist Catherine Kohler Riessman reports in her new book *Divorce Talk* that most of the women she interviewed—but only a few of the men—gave lack of communication as the reason for their divorces. Given the current divorce rate of nearly 50 percent, that amounts to millions of cases in the United States every year—a virtual epidemic of failed conversation.

In my own research, complaints from women about their husbands most often focused not on tangible inequities such as having given up the chance for a career to accompany a husband to his, or doing far more than their share of daily life-support work like cleaning, cooking, social arrangements and errands. Instead, they focused on communication: "He doesn't listen to me," "He doesn't talk to me." I found, as Hacker observed years before, that most wives want their husbands to be, first and foremost, conversational partners, but few husbands share this expectation of their wives.

5   In short, the image that best represents the current crisis is the   5
stereotypical cartoon scene of a man sitting at the breakfast table with a newspaper held up in front of his face, while a woman glares at the back of it, wanting to talk.

Linguistic Battle of the Sexes

How can women and men have such different impressions of communication in marriage? Why the widespread imbalance in their interests and expectations?

In the April [1990] issue of *American Psychologist,* Stanford University's Eleanor Maccoby reports the results of her own and others' research showing that children's development is most influenced by the social structure of peer interactions. Boys and girls tend to play with children of their own gender, and their sex-separate groups have different organizational structures and interactive norms.

I believe these systematic differences in childhood socialization make talk between women and men like cross-cultural communication,

heir to all the attraction and pitfalls of that enticing but difficult en-
terprise. My research on men's and women's conversations uncovered
patterns similar to those described for children's groups.

For women, as for girls, intimacy is the fabric of relationships, and
talk is the thread from which it is woven. Little girls create and maintain friendships by exchanging secrets; similarly, women regard conversation as the cornerstone of friendship. So a woman expects her
husband to be a new and improved version of a best friend. What is
important is not the individual subjects that are discussed but the
sense of closeness, of a life shared, that emerges when people tell their
thoughts, feelings, and impressions.

10   Bonds between boys can be as intense as girls', but they are based   10
less on talking, more on doing things together. Since they don't assume
talk is the cement that binds a relationship, men don't know what kind
of talk women want, and they don't miss it when it isn't there.

Boys' groups are larger, more inclusive, and more hierarchical, so
boys must struggle to avoid the subordinate position in the group.
This may play a role in women's complaints that men don't listen to
them. Some men really don't like to listen, because being the listener
makes them feel one-down, like a child listening to adults or an em-
ployee to a boss.

But often when women tell men, "You aren't listening," and the
men protest, "I am," the men are right. The impression of not listening results from misalignments in the mechanics of conversation. The
misalignment begins as soon as a man and a woman take physical positions. This became clear when I studied videotapes made by psychologist Paul Dorval of children and adults talking to their same-sex
best friends. I found that at every age, the girls and women faced each
other directly, their eyes anchored on each other's faces. At every age,
the boys and men sat at angles to each other and looked elsewhere in
the room, periodically glancing at each other. They were obviously at-
tuned to each other, often mirroring each other's movements. But the
tendency of men to face away can give women the impression they
aren't listening even when they are. A young woman in college was
frustrated: Whenever she told her boyfriend she wanted to talk to him,
he would lie down on the floor, close his eyes, and put his arm over
his face. This signaled to her, "He's taking a nap." But he insisted he
was listening extra hard. Normally, he looks around the room, so he
is easily distracted. Lying down and covering his eyes helped him con-
centrate on what she was saying.

Analogous to the physical alignment that women and men take in conversation is their topical alignment. The girls in my study tended to talk at length about one topic, but the boys tended to jump from topic to topic. The second-grade girls exchanged stories about people they knew. The second-grade boys teased, told jokes, noticed things in the room and talked about finding games to play. The sixth-grade girls talked about problems with a mutual friend. The sixth-grade boys talked about fifty-five different topics, none of which extended over more than a few turns.

Listening to Body Language

Switching topics is another habit that gives women the impression men aren't listening, especially if they switch to a topic about themselves. But the evidence of the tenth-grade boys in my study indicates otherwise. The tenth-grade boys sprawled across their chairs with bodies parallel and eyes straight ahead, rarely looking at each other. They looked as if they were riding in a car, staring out the windshield. But they were talking about their feelings. One boy was upset because a girl had told him he had a drinking problem, and the other was feeling alienated from all his friends.

15   Now, when a girl told a friend about a problem, the friend responded by asking probing questions and expressing agreement and understanding. But the boys dismissed each other's problems. Todd assured Richard that his drinking was "no big problem" because "sometimes you're funny when you're off your butt." And when Todd said he felt left out, Richard responded, "Why should you? You know more people than me."

Women perceive such responses as belittling and unsupportive. But the boys seemed satisfied with them. Whereas women reassure each other by implying, "You shouldn't feel bad because I've had similar experiences," men do so by implying, "You shouldn't feel bad because your problems aren't so bad."

There are even simpler reasons for women's impression that men don't listen. Linguist Lynette Hirschman found that women make more listener-noise, such as "mhm," "uhuh," and "yeah," to show "I'm with you." Men, she found, more often give silent attention. Women who expect a stream of listener-noise interpret silent attention as no attention at all.

Women's conversational habits are as frustrating to men as men's are to women. Men who expect silent attention interpret a stream of listener-noise as overreaction or impatience. Also, when women talk to each other in a close, comfortable setting, they often overlap, finish each other's sentences and anticipate what the other is about to say. This practice, which I call "participatory listenership," is often perceived by men as interruption, intrusion, and lack of attention.

A parallel difference caused a man to complain about his wife, "She just wants to talk about her own point of view. If I show her another view, she gets mad at me." When most women talk to each other, they assume a conversationalist's job is to express agreement and support. But many men see their conversational duty as pointing out the other side of an argument. This is heard as disloyalty by women, and refusal to offer the requisite support. It is not that women don't want to see other points of view, but that they prefer them phrased as suggestions and inquiries rather than as direct challenges.

20   In his book *Fighting for Life,* Walter Ong points out that men use   20 "agonistic," or warlike, oppositional formats to do almost anything; thus discussion becomes debate, and conversation becomes a competitive sport. In contrast, women see conversation as a ritual means of establishing rapport. If Jane tells a problem and June says she has a similar one, they walk away feeling closer to each other. But this attempt at establishing rapport can backfire when used with men. Men take too literally women's ritual "troubles talk," just as women mistake men's ritual challenges for real attack.

The Sounds of Silence

These differences begin to clarify why women and men have such different expectations about communication in marriage. For women, talk creates intimacy. Marriage is an orgy of closeness: you can tell your feelings and thoughts, and still be loved. Their greatest fear is being pushed away. But men live in a hierarchical world, where talk maintains independence and status. They are on guard to protect themselves from being put down and pushed around.

This explains the paradox of the talkative man who said of his silent wife, "She's the talker." In the public setting of a guest lecture, he felt challenged to show his intelligence and display his understanding of the lecture. But at home, where he has nothing to prove and no one to defend against, he is free to remain silent. For his wife, being home means she is free from the worry that something she says might offend someone, or spark disagreement, or appear to be showing off; at home she is free to talk.

The communication problems that endanger marriage can't be fixed by mechanical engineering. They require a new conceptual framework about the role of talk in human relationships. Many of the psychological explanations that have become second nature may not be helpful, because they tend to blame either women (for not being assertive enough) or men (for not being in touch with their feelings). A sociolinguistic approach by which male-female conversation is seen as cross-cultural communication allows us to understand the problem and forge solutions without blaming either party.

Once the problem is understood, improvement comes naturally, as it did to the young woman and her boyfriend who seemed to go to sleep when she wanted to talk. Previously, she had accused him of not listening, and he had refused to change his behavior, since that would be admitting fault. But then she learned about and explained to him the differences in women's and men's habitual ways of aligning themselves in conversation. The next time she told him she wanted to talk, he began, as usual, by lying down and covering his eyes. When the familiar negative reaction bubbled up, she reassured herself that he really was listening. But then he sat up and looked at her. Thrilled, she asked why. He said, "You like me to look at you when we talk, so I'll try to do it." Once he saw their differences as cross-cultural rather than right and wrong, he independently altered his behavior.

25 Women who feel abandoned and deprived when their husbands 25 won't listen to or report daily news may be happy to discover their husbands trying to adapt once they understand the place of small talk in women's relationships. But if their husbands don't adapt, the women may still be comforted that for men, this is not a failure of intimacy. Accepting the difference, the wives may look to their friends or family for that kind of talk. And husbands who can't provide it shouldn't feel their wives have made unreasonable demands. Some couples will still decide to divorce, but at least their decisions will be based on realistic expectations.

In these times of resurgent ethnic conflicts, the world desperately needs cross-cultural understanding. Like charity, successful cross-cultural communication should begin at home.

Questions on Meaning

1. What do men generally want out of conversation? What do women want?
2. Describe the differences between men and women in physical position and behavior during conversation with others of the same sex. What are the differences in how men and women speak?
3. Does Tannen argue that men and women should both try to change so that there are no differences anymore in conversational styles? If so, why? If not, what is her solution?

Questions on Rhetorical Strategy and Style

1. Examine how Tannen uses the rhetorical strategy of comparison and contrast to describe and explain the differences between men and women. How balanced is her analysis?
2. Tannen also uses examples to support and develop her points about how men and women communicate differently. Without rereading, how many different examples can you recall about such differences?
3. At the end of the essay Tannen switches from an emphasis that has been mostly descriptive to one that briefly argues a position. Evaluate the effectiveness of her concluding argument about how men and women should try to understand each other and adapt. What might make her argument stronger?

Writing Assignments

1. Tannen writes of couples who have apparently been married at least a little while, but whose problems are moving them toward divorce. Speculate about a topic she does not discuss: how couples might act and converse differently when they are first dating and forming a relationship. If their conversational styles are the same even early on, enough to cause divorce later on, how do they overcome these problems at first and get married? Or if you think people's conversational styles change after they have been married a while, what causes that change?
2. Tannen generalizes about communication differences between all males and females, even though she writes primarily about married couples. How much do you think her observations apply to single people in your own age group? Go to a place where you can

easily observe apparently single people near your age. Observe at least three conversations: one between two males, one between two females, and one between a male and a female. Take note of behaviors such as physical position, the amount of eye contact, how long each person seems to speak, and so on. Then write an essay presenting your findings.

Being a Man

Paul Theroux

Paul Theroux (1941–) divides his time between England and his native Massachusetts. He has written novels, including the well-regarded The Mosquito Coast; *short stories which were recently collected in his* The Collected Stories *(1997); and many magazine articles. In this essay he explores with vengeful enthusiasm the stereotypical social role reserved for American males.*

1 There is a pathetic sentence in the chapter "Fetishism" in Dr. Norman Cameron's book *Personality Development and Psychopathology.* It goes, "Fetishists are nearly always men; and the commonest fetish is a woman's shoe," I cannot read that sentence without thinking that it is just one more awful thing about being a man—and perhaps it is an important thing to know about us.

 I have always disliked being a man. The whole idea of manhood in America is pitiful, in my opinion. This version of masculinity is a little like having to wear an ill-fitting coat for one's entire life (by contrast, I imagine femininity to be an oppressive sense of nakedness). Even the expression "Be a man!" strikes me as insulting and abusive. It means: Be stupid, be unfeeling, obedient, soldierly and stop thinking. Man means "manly"—how can one think about men without considering the terrible ambition of manliness? And yet it is part of every man's life. It is a hideous and crippling lie; it not only insists on difference and connives at superiority, it is also by its very nature destructive—emotionally damaging and socially harmful.

 The youth who is subverted, as most are, into believing in the masculine ideal is effectively separated from women and he spends the rest of his life finding women a riddle and a nuisance. Of course, there is a female version of this male affliction. It begins with mothers encouraging little girls to say (to other adults) "Do you like my new dress?" In a sense, little girls are traditionally urged to please adults with a kind of coquettishness, while boys are enjoined to behave like monkeys towards each other. The nine-year-old coquette proceeds to become womanish in a subtle power game in which she learns to be sexually indispensable, socially decorative and always alert to a man's sense of inadequacy.

Femininity—being lady-like—implies needing a man as witness and seducer; but masculinity celebrates the exclusive company of men. That is why it is so grotesque; and that is also why there is no manliness without inadequacy—because it denies men the natural friendship of women.

5   It is very hard to imagine any concept of manliness that does not belittle women, and it begins very early. At an age when I wanted to meet girls—let's say the treacherous years of thirteen to sixteen—I was told to take up a sport, get more fresh air, join the Boy Scouts, and I was urged not to read so much. It was the 1950s and if you asked too many questions about sex you were sent to camp—boy's camp, of course: the nightmare. Nothing is more unnatural or prison-like than a boy's camp, but if it were not for them we would have no Elks' Lodges, no pool rooms, no boxing matches, no Marines.

And perhaps no sports as we know them. Everyone is aware of how few in number are the athletes who behave like gentlemen. Just as high school basketball teaches you how to be a poor loser, the manly attitude towards sports seems to be little more than a recipe for creating bad marriages, social misfits, moral degenerates, sadists, latent rapists and just plain louts. I regard high school sports as a drug far worse than marijuana, and it is the reason that the average tennis champion, say, is a pathetic oaf.

Any objective study would find the quest for manliness essentially right-wing, puritanical, cowardly, neurotic and fueled largely by a fear of women. It is also certainly philistine. There is no book-hater like a Little League coach. But indeed all the creative arts are obnoxious to the manly ideal, because at their best the arts are pursued by uncompetitive and essentially solitary people. It makes it very hard for a creative youngster, for any boy who expresses the desire to be alone seems to be saying that there is something wrong with him.

It ought to be clear by now that I have something of an objection to the way we turn boys into men. It does not surprise me that when the President of the United States has his customary weekend off he dresses like a cowboy—it is both a measure of his insecurity and his willingness to please. In many ways, American culture does little more for a man than prepare him for modeling clothes in the L. L. Bean catalogue. I take this as a personal insult because for many years I found it impossible to admit to myself that I wanted to be a writer. It was my guilty secret, because being a writer was incompatible with being a man.

There are people who might deny this, but that is because the American writer, typically, has been so at pains to prove his manliness that we have come to see literariness and manliness as mingled qualities. But first there was a fear that writing was not a manly profession—indeed, not a profession at all. (The paradox in American letters is that it has always been easier for a woman to write and for a man to be published.) Growing up, I had thought of sports as wasteful and humiliating, and the idea of manliness was a bore. My wanting to become a writer was not a flight from that oppressive role-playing, but I quickly saw that it was at odds with it. Everything in stereotyped manliness goes against the life of the mind. The Hemingway personality is too tedious to go into here, and in any case his exertions are well-known, but certainly it was not until this aberrant behavior was examined by feminists in the 1960s that any male writer dared question the pugnacity in Hemingway's fiction. All the bullfighting and arm wrestling and elephant shooting diminished Hemingway as a writer, but it is consistent with a prevailing attitude in American writing: one cannot be a male writer without first proving that one is a man.

10 It is normal in America for a man to be dismissive or even some what apologetic about being a writer. Various factors make it easier. There is a heartiness about journalism that makes it acceptable—journalism is the manliest form of American writing and, therefore, the profession the most independent-minded women seek (yes, it is an illusion, but that is my point). Fiction-writing is equated with a kind of dispirited failure and is only manly when it produces wealth—money is masculinity. So is drinking. Being a drunkard is another assertion, if misplaced, of manliness. The American male writer is traditionally proud of his heavy drinking. But we are also a very literal-minded people. A man proves his manhood in America in old-fashioned ways. He kills lions, like Hemingway; or he hunts ducks,

like Nathanael West; or he makes pronouncements like, "A man should carry enough knife to defend himself with," as James Jones once said to a *Life* interviewer. Or he says he can drink you under the table. But even tiny drunken William Faulkner loved to mount a horse and go fox hunting, and Jack Kerouac roistered up and down Manhattan in a lumberjack shirt (and spent every night of *The Subterraneans* with his mother in Queens). And we are familiar with the lengths to which Norman Mailer is prepared, in his endearing way, to prove that he is just as much a monster as the next man.

When the novelist John Irving was revealed as a wrestler, people took him to be a very serious writer; and even a bubble reputation like Eric (*Love Story*) Segal's was enhanced by the news that he ran the marathon in a respectable time. How surprised we would be if Joyce Carol Oates were revealed as a sumo wrestler or Joan Didion active in pumping iron. "Lives in New York City with her three children" is the typical woman writer's biographical note, for just as the male writer must prove he has achieved a sort of muscular manhood, the woman writer—or rather her publicists—must prove her motherhood.

There would be no point in saying any of this if it were not generally accepted that to be a man is somehow—even now in feminist-influenced America—a privilege. It is on the contrary an unmerciful and punishing burden. Being a man is bad enough; being manly is appalling (in this sense, women's lib has done much more for men than for women). It is the sinister silliness of men's fashions, and a clubby attitude in the arts. It is the subversion of good students. It is the so-called "Dress Code" of the Ritz-Carlton Hotel in Boston, and it is the institutionalized cheating in college sports. It is the most primitive insecurity.

And this is also why men often object to feminism but are afraid to explain why: of course women have a justified grievance, but most men believe—and with reason—that their lives are just as bad.

Questions on Meaning

1. List the negative qualities of the American male that Theroux mentions. Does the list correspond to reality as you know it?
2. What are the losses to men who try to live up to the stereotype Theroux describes?

Questions on Rhetorical Strategy and Style

1. This piece of writing could be called a diatribe—a bitter and abusive denunciation. Locate and list particular word choices that suggest bitterness. What experiences do you think are behind Theroux's feelings?
2. Theroux's intention here is primarily to express his opinion rather than to persuade an audience. If he were going to rewrite this essay with a more persuasive intent, which points would be the most important to retain? Which would he have to cut out?
3. What are the more positive meanings of the expression, "Be a man"?

Writing Assignments

1. Write an essay in which you define the concept of "man" based on the men you know. List some of the more important and representative men in your life and note the qualities they share. Illustrate your discussion with descriptions of the men's belief and behavior.
2. Write an essay that defines the concept of "man" by dividing it into types of men. Your typology may be based on age or generation (e.g., the middle-aged man, the man of the nineties), geography (the Western man, the urban man), tastes (the conservative man, the GQ man), or some other set of factors that seems important to you.

Motherhood: Who Needs It?

Betty Rollin

*Betty Rollin (1936–) was born in New York City. A grad-
uate of Sarah Lawrence College (B.A., 1957), Rollin has
worked for* Vogue, Look, *NBC News, and ABC Night-
line. Her books include* I Thee Wed *(1958),* Mothers are
Funnier than Children *(1964),* The Non-Drinker's
Drink Book *(1966),* First You Cry *(1976), and* Last
Wish *(1985). This essay, published in* Look *in 1970, de-
bunks what Rollin calls the "motherhood myth."*

1   Motherhood is in trouble, and it ought to be. A rude question is long overdue: Who needs it? The answer used to be
(1) society and (2) women. But now, with the impending
horrors of overpopulation, society desperately *doesn't* need it. And
women don't need it either. Thanks to the Motherhood Myth—the
idea that having babies is something that all normal women instinc-
tively want and need and will enjoy doing—they just *think* they do.

The notion that the maternal wish and the activity of mothering
are instinctive or biologically predestined is baloney. Try asking most sociologists, psychologists, psychoanalysts, biologists—many of whom are
mothers—about motherhood being instinctive: it's like asking department store presidents if their Santa Clauses are real. "Motherhood—
instinctive?" shouts distinguished sociologist/author Dr. Jessie Bernard.
"Biological destiny? Forget biology! If it were biology, people would die
from not doing it."

"Women don't need to be mothers any more than they need
spaghetti," says Dr. Richard Rabkin, a New York psychiatrist. "But if
you're in a world where everyone is eating spaghetti, thinking they

need it and want it, you will think so too. Romance has really contaminated science. So-called instincts have to do with stimulation. They are not things that well up inside of you."

"When a woman says with feeling that she craved her baby from within, she is putting into biological language what is psychological," says University of Michigan psychoanalyst and motherhood-researcher Dr. Frederick Wyatt. "There are no instincts," says Dr. William Goode, president-elect of the American Sociological Association. "There are reflexes, like eye-blinking, and drives, like sex. There is no innate drive for children. Otherwise, the enormous cultural pressures that there are to reproduce wouldn't exist. There are no cultural pressures to sell you on getting your hand out of the fire."

5   There are, to be sure, biologists and others who go on about bio   5
logical destiny, that is, the innate or instinctive goal of motherhood. (At the turn of the century, even good old capitalism was explained by a theorist as "the *instinct* of acquisitiveness.") And many psychoanalysts will hold the Freudian view that women feel so rotten about not having a penis that they are necessarily propelled into the child-wish to replace the missing organ. Psychoanalysts also make much of the psychological need to repeat what one's parent of the same sex has done. Since every woman has a mother, it is considered normal to wish to imitate one's mother by being a mother.

There is, surely, a wish to pass on love if one has received it, but to insist women must pass it on in the same way is like insisting that every man whose father is a gardener has to be a gardener. One dissenting psychoanalyst says, simply, "There is a wish to comply with one's biology, yes, but we needn't and sometimes we shouldn't." (Interestingly, the woman who has been the greatest contributor to child therapy and who has probably given more to children than anyone alive is Dr. Anna Freud, Freud's magnificent daughter, who is not a mother.)

Anyway, what an expert cast of hundreds is telling us is, simply, that biological *possibility* and desire are not the same as biological *need.* Women have childbearing equipment. To choose not to use the equipment is no more blocking what is instinctive than it is for a man who, muscles or no, chooses not to be a weight lifter.

So much for the wish. What about the "instinctive" *activity* of mothering? One animal study shows that when a young member of a species is put in a cage, say, with an older member of the same species, the latter will act in a protective, "maternal" way. But that goes for both males and females who have been "mothered" themselves. And studies indicate that a human baby will also respond to whoever is around playing mother—even if it's father. Margaret Mead and many others frequently point out that mothering can be a fine occupation, if you want it, for either sex. Another experiment with monkeys who were brought up without mothers found them lacking in maternal behavior toward their own offspring. A similar study showed that monkeys brought up without other monkeys of the opposite sex had no interest in mating—all of which suggests that both mothering and mating behavior are learned, not instinctual. And, to turn the cart (or the baby carriage) around, baby ducks who lovingly follow their mothers seemed, in the mother's absence, to just as lovingly follow wooden ducks or even vacuum cleaners.

If motherhood isn't instinctive, when and why, then, was the Motherhood Myth born? Until recently, the entire question of maternal motivation was academic. Sex, like it or not, meant babies. Not that there haven't always been a lot of interesting contraceptive tries. But until the creation of the diaphragm in the 1880's, the birth of babies was largely unavoidable. And, generally speaking, nobody really seemed to mind. For one thing, people tend to be sort of good sports about what seems to be inevitable. For another, in the past, the population needed beefing up. Mortality rates were high, and agricultural cultures, particularly, have always needed children to help out. So because it "just happened" and because it was needed, motherhood was assumed to be innate.

10   Originally, it was the word of God that got the ball rolling with   10
"Be fruitful and multiply," a practical suggestion, since the only people around then were Adam and Eve. But in no time, supermoralists like St. Augustine changed the tone of the message: "Intercourse, even with one's legitimate wife, is unlawful and wicked where the conception of the offspring is prevented," he, we assume, thundered. And the Roman Catholic position was thus cemented. So then and now, procreation took on a curious value among people who viewed (and view) the pleasures of sex as sinful. One could partake in the sinful pleasure, but feel vindicated by the ensuing birth. Motherhood cleaned up sex. Also, it cleaned up women, who have always been considered somewhat evil, because of Eve's transgression (". . . but the woman was deceived and became a transgressor. Yet woman will be saved through

bearing children . . . ," I Timothy, 2:14–15), and somewhat dirty because of menstruation.

And so, based on need, inevitability, and pragmatic fantasy—the Myth *worked,* from society's point of view—the Myth grew like corn in Kansas. And society reinforced it with both laws and propaganda—laws that made woman a chattel, denied her education and personal mobility, and madonna propaganda that she was beautiful and wonderful doing it and it was all beautiful and wonderful to do. (One rarely sees a madonna washing dishes.)

In fact, the Myth persisted—breaking some kind of record for long-lasting fallacies—until something like yesterday. For as the truth about the Myth trickled in—as women's rights increased, as women gradually got the message that it was certainly possible for them to do most things that men did, that they live longer, that their brains were not tinier—then, finally, when the really big news rolled in, that they could choose whether or not to be mothers—what happened? The Motherhood Myth soared higher than ever. As Betty Friedan made oh-so-clear in *The Feminine Mystique,* the '40's and '50's produced a group of ladies who not only had babies as if they were going out of style (maybe they were) but, as never before, they turned motherhood into a cult. First, they wallowed in the aesthetics of it all—natural childbirth and nursing became maternal musts. Like heavy-bellied ostriches, they grounded their heads in the sands of motherhood, only coming up for air to say how utterly happy and fulfilled they were. But, as Mrs. Friedan says only too plainly, they weren't. The Myth galloped on, moreover, long after making babies had turned from practical asset to liability for both individual parents and society. With the average cost of a middle-class child figured conservatively at $30,000 (not including college), any parent knows that the only people who benefit economically from children are manufacturers of consumer goods. Hence all those gooey motherhood commercials. And the Myth gathered momentum long after sheer numbers, while not yet extinguishing us, have made us intensely uncomfortable. Almost all of our societal problems, from minor discomforts like traffic to major ones like hunger, the population people keep reminding us, have to do with there being too many people. And who suffers most? The kids who have been so mindlessly brought into the world, that's who. They are the ones who have to cope with all of the difficult and dehumanizing conditions brought on by overpopulation. They are the ones who have to cope with the psychological nausea of feeling unneeded by society. That's not the only reason for drugs, but, surely, it's a leading contender,

Unfortunately, the population curbers are tripped up by a romantic, stubborn, ideological hurdle. How can birth-control programs really be effective as long as the concept of glorious motherhood remains unchanged? (Even poor old Planned Parenthood has to euphemize—why not Planned Unparenthood?) Particularly among the poor, motherhood is one of the few inherently positive institutions that are accessible. As Berkeley demographer Judith Blake points out, "Poverty-oriented birth control programs do not make sense as a welfare measure . . . as long as existing pronatalist policies . . . encourage mating, pregnancy, and the care, support, and rearing of children." Or, she might have added, as long as the less-than-idyllic child-rearing part of motherhood remains "in small print."

Sure, motherhood gets dumped on sometimes: Philip Wylie's Momism got going in the '40's and Philip Roth's *Portnoy's Complaint* did its best to turn rancid the chicken-soup concept of Jewish motherhood. But these are viewed as the sour cries of a black humorist here, a malcontent there. Everyone shudders, laughs, but it's like the mouse and the elephant joke. Still, the Myth persists. Last April, a Brooklyn woman was indicted on charges of manslaughter and negligent homicide—eleven children died in a fire in a building she owned and criminally neglected—"But," sputtered her lawyer, "my client, Mrs. Breslow, is a mother, a grandmother, and a great grandmother!"

15 Most remarkably, the Motherhood Myth persists in the face of the 15 most overwhelming maternal unhappiness and incompetence. If reproduction were merely superfluous and expensive, if the experience were as rich and rewarding as the cliché would have us believe, if it were a predominantly joyous trip for everyone riding—mother, father, child—then the going everybody-should-have-two-children plan would suffice. Certainly, there are a lot of joyous mothers, and their children and (sometimes, not necessarily) their husbands reflect their joy. But a lot of evidence suggests that for more women than anyone wants to admit, motherhood can be miserable. ("If it weren't," says one psychiatrist wryly, "the world wouldn't be in the mess it's in.")

There is a remarkable statistical finding from a recent study of Dr. Bernard's, comparing the mental illness and unhappiness of married mothers and single women. The latter group, it turned out, was both markedly less sick and overtly more happy. Of course, it's not easy to measure slippery attitudes like happiness. "Many women have achieved a kind of reconciliation—a conformity," says Dr. Bernard,

> that they interpret as happiness. Since feminine happiness is supposed to lie in devoting one's life to one's husband and children, they do that; so ipso facto, they assume they are happy. And for many women, untrained for independence and "processed" for motherhood, they find their state far preferable to the alternatives, which don't really exist.

Also, unhappy mothers are often loath to admit it. For one thing, if in society's view not to be a mother is to be a freak, not to be a *blissful* mother is to be a witch. Besides, unlike a disappointing marriage, disappointing motherhood cannot be terminated by divorce. Of course, none of that stops such a woman from expressing her dissatisfaction in a variety of ways. Again, it is not only she who suffers but her husband and children as well. Enter the harridan housewife, the carping shrew. The realities of motherhood can turn women into terrible people. And, judging from the 50,000 cases of child abuse in the U.S. each year, some are worse than terrible.

In some cases, the unpleasing realities of motherhood begin even before the beginning. In *Her Infinite Variety,* Morton Hunt describes young married women pregnant for the first time as "very likely to be frightened and depressed, masking these feelings in order not to be considered contemptible. The arrival of pregnancy interrupts a pleasant dream of motherhood and awakens them to the realization that they have too little money, or not enough space, or unresolved marital problems. . . ."

The following are random quotes from interviews with some mothers in Ann Arbor, Mich., who described themselves as reasonably happy. They all had positive things to say about their children, although when asked about the best moment of their day, they all confessed it was when the children were in bed. Here is the rest:

> Suddenly I had to devote myself to the child totally. I was under the illusion that the baby was going to fit into my life, and I found that I had to switch my life and my schedule to fit him. You think, "I'm in love, I'll get married, and we'll have a baby." First there's two, then three, it's simple and romantic. You don't even think about the work. . . .

You never get away from the responsibility. Even when you leave the children with a sitter, you are not out from under the pressure of the responsibility. . . .

I hate ironing their pants and doing their underwear, and they never put their clothes in the laundry basket. . . . As they get older, they make less demands on our time because they're in school, but the demands are greater in forming their values. . . . Best moment of the day is when all the children are in bed. . . . The worst time of the day is 4 P.M., when you have to get dinner started, the kids are tired, hungry and crabby—everybody wants to talk to you about their day . . . your day is only half over.

Once a mother, the responsibility and concern for my children became so encompassing. . . . It took me a great deal of will to keep up other parts of my personality. . . . To me, motherhood gets harder as they get older because you have less control. . . . In an abstract sense, I'd have, several. . . . In the nonabstract, I would not have any. . . .

I had anticipated that the baby would sleep and eat, sleep and eat. Instead, the experience was overwhelming. I really had not thought particularly about what motherhood would mean in a realistic sense. I want to do other things, like to become involved in things that are worthwhile—I don't mean women's clubs—but I don't have the physical energy to go out in the evenings. I feel like I'm missing something . . . the experience of being somewhere with people and having them talking about something—something that's going on in the world.

Every grownup person expects to pay a price for his pleasures, but seldom is the price as vast as the one endured "however happily" by most mothers. We have mentioned the literal cost factor. But what does that mean? For middle-class American women, it means a life style with severe and usually unimagined limitations; i.e., life in the suburbs, because who can afford three bedrooms in the city? And what do suburbs mean? For women, suburbs mean other women and children and leftover peanut-butter sandwiches and car pools and seldom-seen husbands. Even the Feminine Mystiqueniks—the housewives who finally admitted that their lives behind brooms (OK, electric brooms) were driving them crazy—were loath to trace their predicament to their children. But it is simply a fact that a childless married woman has no child-work and little housework. She can live in a city, or, if she still chooses the suburbs or the country, she can leave on the commuter train with her husband if she wants to. Even the most ardent job-seeking mother will find little in the way of great opportunities in Scarsdale. Besides, by the time she wakes up, she usually lacks both the preparation for the outside world and the self-confidence to get it. You will say there are plenty of city-dwelling working mothers. But most of those women do additional-funds-for-the-family kind of work, not the interesting career kind that takes plugging during childbearing years.

20   Nor is it a bed of petunias for the mother who does make it professionally. Says writer-critic Marya Mannes: 20

> *If the creative woman has children, she must pay for this indulgence with a long burden of guilt, for her life will be split three ways between them and her husband and her work. . . . No woman with any heart can compose a paragraph when her child is in trouble. . . . The creative woman has no wife to protect her from intrusion. A man at his desk in a room with closed door is a man at work. A woman at a desk in any room is available.*

Speaking of jobs, do remember that mothering, salary or not, is a job. Even those who can afford nurses to handle the nitty-gritty still need to put out emotionally. "Well-cared-for" neurotic rich kids are not exactly unknown in our society. One of the more absurd aspects of the Myth is the underlying assumption that, since most women are biologically equipped to bear children, they are psychologically, mentally, emotionally, and technically equipped (or interested) to rear them. Never mind happiness. To assume that such an exacting, consuming, and important task is something almost all women are equipped to do is far more dangerous and ridiculous than assuming that everyone with vocal chords should seek a career in the opera.

A major expectation of the Myth is that children make a not-so-hot marriage hotter, or a hot marriage, hotter still. Yet almost every available study indicates that childless marriages are far happier. One of the biggest, of 850 couples, was conducted by Dr. Harold Feldman of Cornell University, who states his finding in no uncertain terms: "Those couples with children had a significantly lower level of marital satisfaction than did those without children." Some of the reasons are obvious. Even the most adorable children make for additional demands, complications, and hardships in the lives of even the most loving parents. If a woman feels disappointed and trapped in her mother role, it is bound to affect her marriage in any number of ways: she may take out her frustrations directly on her husband, or she may count on him too heavily for what she feels she is missing in her daily life.

". . . You begin to grow away from your husband," says one of the Michigan ladies. "He's working on his career and you're working on your family. But you both must gear your lives to the children. You do things the children enjoy, more than things you might enjoy." More subtle and possibly more serious is what motherhood may do to a woman's sexuality. Often when the stork flies in, sexuality flies out. Both in the emotional minds of some women and in the minds of their husbands, when a woman becomes a mother, she stops being a woman. It's not only that motherhood may destroy her physical attractiveness, but its madonna concept may destroy her *feelings* of sexuality.

And what of the payoff? Usually, even the most self-sacrificing of maternal self-sacrificers expects a little something back. Gratified parents are not unknown to the Western world, but there are probably at least just as many who feel, to put it crudely, shortchanged. The experiment mentioned earlier—where the baby ducks followed vacuum cleaners instead of their mothers—indicates that what passes for love from baby to mother is merely a rudimentary kind of object attachment. Without necessarily feeling like a Hoover, a lot of women become disheartened because babies and children are not only not interesting to talk to (not everyone thrills at the wonders of da-da-ma-ma talk) but they are generally not empathetic, considerate people. Even the nicest children are not capable of empathy, surely a major ingredient of love, until they are much older. Sometimes they're never capable of it. Dr. Wyatt says that often, in later years particularly, when most of the "returns" are in, it is the "good mother" who suffers most of all. It is then she must face a reality: The child—the appendage with her genes—is not an appendage, but a separate person. What's more, he or she may be a separate person who doesn't even like her—or whom she doesn't really like.

25 So if the music is lousy, how come everyone's dancing? Because the 25 motherhood minuet is taught freely from birth, and whether or not she has rhythm or likes the music, every woman is expected to do it. Indeed, she *wants* to do it. Little girls start learning what to want—and what to be—when they are still in their cribs. Dr. Miriam Keiffer, a

young social psychologist at Bensalem, the Experimental College of Fordham University, points to studies showing that

> *at six months of age, mothers are already treating their baby girls and boys quite differently. For instance, mothers have been found to touch, comfort, and talk to their females more. If these differences can be found at such an early stage, it's not surprising that the end product is as different as it is. What is surprising is that men and women are, in so many ways, similar.*

Some people point to the way little girls play with dolls as proof of their innate motherliness. But remember, little girls are *given* dolls. When Margaret Mead presented some dolls to New Guinea children, it was the boys, not the girls, who wanted to play with them, which they did by crooning lullabies and rocking them in the most maternal fashion.

By the time they reach adolescence, most girls, unconsciously or not, have learned enough about role definition to qualify for a master's degree. In general, the lesson has been that no matter what kind of career thoughts one may entertain, one must, first and foremost, be a wife and mother. A girl's mother is usually her first teacher. As Dr. Goode says, "A woman is not only taught by society to have a child; she is taught to have a child who will have a child." A woman who has hung her life on the Motherhood Myth will almost always reinforce her young married daughter's early training by pushing for grandchildren. Prospective grandmothers are not the only ones. Husbands, too, can be effective sellers. After all, they have the Fatherhood Myth to cope with. A married man is *supposed* to have children. Often, particularly among Latins, children are a sign of potency. They help him assure the world—and himself—that he is the big man he is supposed to be. Plus, children give him both immortality (whatever that means) and possibly the chance to become more in his lifetime through the accomplishments of his children, particularly his son. (Sometimes it's important, however, for the son to do better, but not *too* much better.)

Friends, too, can be counted on as myth-pushers. Naturally one wants to do what one's friends do. One study, by the way, found a correlation between a woman's fertility and that of her three closest friends. The negative sell comes into play here, too. We have seen what the concept of non-mother means (cold, selfish, unwomanly, abnormal). In practice, particularly in the suburbs, it can mean, simply, exclusion—both from child-centered activities (that is, most activities) and child-centered conversations (that is, most conversations). It can also mean being the butt of a lot of unfunny jokes. ("Whaddya waiting for? An immaculate conception? Ha ha.") Worst of all, it can mean being an object of pity.

In case she's escaped all those pressures (that is, if she was brought up in a cave), a young married woman often wants a baby just so that she'll (1) have something to do (motherhood is better than clerk/typist, which is often the only kind of job she can get, since little more has been expected of her and, besides, her boss also expects her to leave and be a mother); (2) have something to hug and possess, to be needed by and have power over; and (3) have something to *be*—e.g., a baby's mother. Motherhood affords an instant identity. First, through wifehood, you are somebody's wife; then you are somebody's mother. Both give not only identity and activity, but status and stardom of a kind. During pregnancy, a woman can look forward to the kind of attention and pampering she may not ever have gotten or may never otherwise get. Some women consider birth the biggest accomplishment of their lives, which may be interpreted as saying not much for the rest of their lives. As Dr. Goode says, "It's like the gambler who may know the roulette wheel is crooked, but it's the only game in town." Also, with motherhood, the feeling of accomplishment is immediate. It is really much faster and easier to make a baby than paint a painting, or write a book, or get to the point of accomplishment in a job. It is also easier in a way to shift focus from self-development to child development—particularly since, for women, self-development is considered selfish. Even unwed mothers may achieve a feeling of this kind. (As we have seen, little thought is given to the aftermath.) And, again, since so many women are underdeveloped as people, they feel that, besides children, they have little else to give—to themselves, their husbands, to their world.

You may ask why then, when the realities do start pouring in, does a woman want to have a second, third, even fourth child? OK, (1) just because reality is pouring in doesn't mean she wants to *face* it. A new baby can help bring back some of the old illusions. Says psychoanalyst Dr. Natalie Shainess, "She may view each successive child as a knight in armor that will rescue her from being a 'bad unhappy mother.' " (2) Next on the horror list of having no children, is having one. It suffices to say that only children are not only OK, they even have a high rate of exceptionality. (3) Both parents usually want at least one child of each sex. The husband, for reasons discussed earlier, probably wants a son. (4) The more children one has, the more of an excuse one has not to develop in any other way.

30 What's the point? A world without children? Of course not. 30 Nothing could be worse or more unlikely. No matter what anyone says in *Look* or anywhere else, motherhood isn't about to go out like a blown bulb, and who says it should? Only the Myth must go out, and now it seems to be dimming.

The younger-generation females who have been reared on the Myth have not rejected it totally, but at least they recognize it can be more loving to children not to have them. And at least they speak of adopting children instead of bearing them. Moreover, since the new nonbreeders are "less hung-up" on ownership, they seem to recognize that if you dig loving children, you don't necessarily have to own one. The end of the Motherhood Myth might make available more loving women (and men!) for those children who already exist.

When motherhood is no longer culturally compulsory, there will, certainly, be less of it. Women are now beginning to think and do more about development of self, of their individual resources. Far from being selfish, such development is probably our only hope. That means more alternatives for women. And more alternatives means more selective, better, happier, motherhood—and childhood and hus-bandhood (or manhood) and peoplehood. It is not a question of whether or not children are sweet and marvelous to have and rear; the question is, even if that's so, whether or not one wants to pay the price for it. It doesn't make sense any more to pretend that women need ba-bies, when what they really need is themselves. If God were still speak-ing to us in a voice we could hear, even He would probably say, "Be fruitful. Don't multiply."

Questions on Meaning

1. What does Rollins mean by the "Motherhood Myth" and the "Fatherhood Myth"? Why has the "Motherhood Myth" persisted throughout the years? Why does Rollins believe it is beginning to fade?
2. What does Rollins mean by the statement that "among the poor, motherhood is one of the few inherently positive institutions that are accessible"? Why does she quote a demographer as saying that "poverty-oriented birth control programs do not make sense"?
3. What does Rollins say in this 1970 essay about the impact of motherhood and having a meaningful career? How relevant are her comments today?

Questions on Rhetorical Strategy and Style

1. To debunk the "instinctive" nature of motherhood, Rollins cites research performed on animals. How did you react to these studies and how she interpreted them? Explain why you felt they do or do not strengthen her argument.
2. Find where Rollins uses a cause and effect writing strategy to show how the Bible and religion promote the "Motherhood Myth." How does society reinforce the myth?
3. To support her argument, Rollins quotes a number of "reasonably happy" mothers. How effective are these comments? Summarize the general theme of these comments.

Writing Assignments

1. What reasons do *you* see for having children? Compare and contrast your reasons to the various reasons—real and imagined—given by Rollins throughout the essay.
2. Write job descriptions for motherhood and fatherhood. Create a checklist that a prospective mother and prospective father might use to see if they are appropriate candidates for these jobs.
3. Research worldwide population growth predictions for the next 50 years. Write an essay on the ramifications of the predicted population growth, highlighting the problems commonly associated with population growth (food, shelter, disease). Explain why you agree or disagree with the conclusions of researchers. What measures do you feel should be taken to control population growth, if any?

Erotica and Pornography

Gloria Steinem

Gloria Steinem (1934–) was born in Toledo, Ohio, and after graduating from Smith College went on to further studies at the University of Delhi and the University of Calcutta. She began a career in political journalism with her column for New York *magazine in the late 1960s. In 1971 she cofounded* Ms. *magazine and became its editor, a position she held until 1987. Steinem has been a key figure in the feminist movement and has worked with the National Women's Political Caucus and the Women's Action Alliance. She published her first collection of essays and columns,* Outrageous Acts and Everyday Rebellions, *in 1983, followed by* Revolution from Within *(1992) and* Moving Beyond Words *(1994). Her concern for women's rights and equality can be seen in the following essay, which explores one of the ways women's bodies have been exploited.*

1   Human beings are the only animals that experience the same sex drive at times when we can—and cannot—conceive. Just as we developed uniquely human capacities for language, planning, memory, and invention along our evolutionary path, we also developed sexuality as a form of expression; a way of communicating that is separable from our need for sex as a way of perpetuating ourselves. For humans alone, sexuality can be and often is primarily a way of bonding, of giving and receiving pleasure, bridging differentness, discovering sameness, and communicating emotion.

We developed this and other human gifts through our ability to change our environment, adapt physically, and in the long run, to affect our own evolution. But as an emotional result of this spiraling path away from other animals, we seem to alternate between periods of exploring our unique abilities to change new boundaries, and feelings of loneliness in the unknown that we ourselves have created; a fear that sometimes sends us back to the comfort of the animal world by encouraging us to exaggerate our sameness.

The separation of "play" from "work," for instance, is a problem only in the human world. So is the difference between art and nature, or an intellectual accomplishment and a physical one. As a result, we celebrate play, art, and invention as leaps into the unknown; but any imbalance can send us back to nostalgia for our primate past and the conviction that the basics of work, nature, and physical labor are somehow more worthwhile or even moral.

5   In the same way, we have explored our sexuality as separable from   5
conception: a pleasurable, empathetic bridge to strangers of the same species. We have even invented contraception—a skill that has probably existed in some form since our ancestors figured out the process of birth—in order to extend this uniquely human difference. Yet we also have times of atavistic suspicion that sex is not complete—or even legal or intended-by-god—if it cannot end in conception.

No wonder the concepts of "erotica" and "pornography" can be so crucially different, and yet so confused. Both assume that sexuality can be separated from conception, and therefore can be used to carry a personal message. That's a major reason why, even in our current culture, both may be called equally "shocking" or legally "obscene," a word whose Latin derivative means "dirty, containing filth." This gross condemnation of all sexuality that isn't harnessed to childbirth and marriage has been increased by the current backlash against women's progress. Out of fear that the whole patriarchal structure might be upset if women really had the autonomous power to decide our reproductive futures (that is, if we controlled the most basic means of production), right-wing groups are not only denouncing prochoice abortion literature as "pornographic," but are trying to stop the sending of all contraceptive information through the mails by invoking obscenity laws. In fact, Phyllis Schlafly recently denounced the entire Women's Movement as "obscene."

Not surprisingly, this religious, visceral backlash has a secular, intellectual counterpart that relies heavily on applying the "natural" behavior of the animal world to humans. That is questionable in it-self, but these Lionel Tiger-ish studies make their political purpose even more clear in the particular animals they select and the habits they choose to emphasize. The message is that females should accept their "destiny" of being sexually dependent and devote themselves to bearing and rearing their young.

Defending against such reaction in turn leads to another tempta-tion: to merely reverse the terms, and declare that *all* nonprocreative sex is good. In fact, however, this human activity can be as constructive or destructive, moral or immoral, as any other. Sex as communication can send messages as different as life and death; even the origins of "erot-ica" and "pornography" reflect that fact. After all, "erotica" is rooted in *eros* or passionate love, and thus in the idea of positive choice, free will, the yearning for a particular person. (Interestingly, the definition of erotica leaves open the question of gender.) "Pornography" begins with a root meaning "prostitution" or "female captives," thus letting us know that the subject is not mutual love, or love at all, but domination and violence against women. (Though, of course, homosexual pornography may imitate this violence by putting a man in the "feminine" role of victim.) It ends with a root meaning "writing about" or "description of" which puts still more distance between subject and object, and replaces a spontaneous yearning for closeness with objectification and a voyeur.

The difference is clear in the words. It becomes even more so by example.

10   Look at any photo or film of people making love; really making   10
love. The images may be diverse, but there is usually a sensuality and touch and warmth, an acceptance of bodies and nerve endings. There is always a spontaneous sense of people who are there because they *want* to be, out of shared pleasure.

Now look at any depiction of sex in which there is clear force, or an unequal power that spells coercion. It may be very blatant, with weapons or torture or bondage, wounds and bruises, some clear humil-iation, or an adult's sexual power being used over a child. It may be much more subtle: a physical attitude of conqueror and victim, the use of race or class difference to imply the same thing, perhaps a very un-equal nudity, with one person exposed and vulnerable while the other is clothed. In either case, there is no sense of equal choice or equal power.

The first is erotic: a mutually pleasurable, sexual expression be-tween people who have enough power to be there by positive choice.

117

It may or may not strike a sense-memory in the viewer, or be creative enough to make the unknown seem real; but it doesn't require us to identify with a conqueror or a victim. It is truly sensuous, and may give us a contagion of pleasure.

The second is pornographic: its message is violence, dominance, and conquest. It is sex being used to reinforce some inequality, or to create one, or to tell us the lie that pain and humiliation (ours or someone else's) are really the same as pleasure. If we are to feel anything, we must identify with conqueror or victim. That means we can only experience pleasure through the adoption of some degree of sadism or masochism. It also means that we may feel diminished by the role of conqueror, or enraged, humiliated, and vengeful by sharing identity with the victim.

Perhaps one could simply say that erotica is about sexuality, but pornography is about power and sex-as-weapon—in the same way we have come to understand that rape is about violence, and not really about sexuality at all.

15   Yes, it's true that there are women who have been forced by vio-   15
lent families and dominating men to confuse love with pain; so much so that they have become masochists. (A fact that in no way excuses those who administer such pain.) But the truth is that, for most women—and for men with enough humanity to imagine themselves into the predicament of women—true pornography could serve as aversion therapy for sex.

Of course, there will always be personal differences about what is and is not erotic, and there may be cultural differences for a long time to come. Many women feel that sex makes them vulnerable and therefore may continue to need more sense of personal connection and safety before allowing any erotic feelings. We now find competence and expertise erotic in men, but that may pass as we develop those qualities in ourselves. Men, on the other hand, may continue to feel less vulnerable, and therefore more open to such potential danger as sex with strangers. As some men replace the need for submission from childlike women with the pleasure of cooperation from equals, they may find a partner's competence to be erotic, too.

Such group changes plus individual differences will continue to be reflected in sexual love between people of the same gender, as well as between women and men. The point is not to dictate sameness, but to discover ourselves and each other through sexuality that is an exploring, pleasurable, empathetic part of our lives; a human sexuality that is unchained both from unwanted pregnancies and from violence.

But that is a hope, not a reality. At the moment, fear of change is increasing both the indiscriminate repression of all nonprocreative sex in the religious and "conservative" male world, and the pornographic vengeance against women's sexuality in the secular world of "liberal" and "radical" men. It's almost futuristic to debate what is and is not truly erotic, when many women are again being forced into compulsory motherhood, and the number of pornographic murders, tortures, and woman-hating images are on the increase in both popular culture and real life.

It's a familiar division: wife or whore, "good" woman who is constantly vulnerable to pregnancy or "bad" woman who is unprotected from violence. *Both* roles would be upset if we were to control our own sexuality. And that's exactly what we must do.

In spite of all our atavistic suspicions and training for the "natural" role of motherhood, we took up the complicated battle for reproductive freedom. Our bodies had borne the health burden of endless births and poor abortions, and we had a greater motive for separating sexuality and conception.

Now we have to take up the equally complex burden of explaining that all nonprocreative sex is *not* alike. We have a motive: our right to a uniquely human sexuality, and sometimes even to survival. As it is, our bodies have too rarely been enough our own to develop erotica in our own lives, much less in art and literature. And our bodies have too often been the objects of pornography and the woman-hating, violent practice that it preaches. Consider also our spirits that break a little each time we see ourselves in chains or full labial display for the conquering male viewer, bruised or on our knees, screaming a real or pretended pain to delight the sadist, pretending to enjoy what we don't enjoy, to be blind to the images of our sisters that really haunt us—humiliated often enough ourselves by the truly obscene idea that sex and the domination of women must be combined.

Sexuality *is* human, free, separate—and so are we.

But until we untangle the lethal confusion of sex with violence, there will be more pornography and less erotica. There will be little murders in our beds—and very little love.

Questions on Meaning

1. How does Steinem define "erotica"? What is her definition for "pornography"?
2. Why does Steinem discuss contraception and abortion rights in this essay? How do they fit into the larger context in which she discusses erotica?
3. What does she mean by the "little murders in our beds" in the final sentence? How is this related to a key theme throughout the essay?

Questions on Rhetorical Strategy and Style

1. For whom is Steinem writing? Identify the "we" of the essay. How does this identification between the writer and reader strengthen her message in the essay?
2. Make a list of adjectives that describe Steinem's sentence-level style. How vivid and persuasive is she in her writing? Compare her style with that of other feminist writers you have read.
3. Some men (and women) have found Steinem's style polarizing and confrontational. Are there any points in this essay at which she seems to lose objectivity or go too far in her generalizations about men and women—to the point of unjustifiably criticizing all men? If so, what is her point in doing so?

Writing Assignments

1. Steinem makes it seem a simple process to distinguish between erotica and pornography, since her definitions and examples are so clear-cut. Courts have had great difficulties, however, in applying antipornography laws, because sometimes the difference is not so clear. Using a hypothetical example or a real example from a case you may know of, explain how in some cases there may seem to be an overlap between erotica and pornography.
2. Steinem writes that most pornography involves images of men in domination over women— showing women in vulnerable, power-less roles—with women's bodies "the objects of pornography." Erotica, on the other hand, is "mutually pleasurable" and "truly sensuous" and not degrading to women. Interestingly, however, most erotic literature and art has been produced by men, with women's bodies the object. One need only consider the long art

tradition of female "nudes." Should there be a balance of the sexes for erotica to exist in the positive way in which Steinem defines it? Would she seem to be arguing for artistic display of men and women making love? Do some research about what is usually meant by "erotica" and write an essay in which you describe (or argue for or against) a feminist version of erotica.

The Rites of Sisterhood

Naomi Wolf

Naomi Wolf (1962–) was born in San Francisco, graduated from Yale University and attended Oxford University as a Rhodes Scholar. As a teenager, Wolf nearly died from anorexia, so that, when she wrote The Beauty Myth: How Images of Beauty Are Used Against Women *(1990), her perspective was both personal and intellectual. She has written for magazines such as* Glamour *and* Ms. *and has won prizes for her poetry. She has continued her interest in feminist issues with* Fire With Fire: The New Female Power and How It Will Change the Twenty-First Century *(1993),* Promiscuities: The Struggle for Womanhood *(1997), and* Misconceptions: Truths, Lies, and the Unexpected on the Journey to Motherhood *(2000). In a 2004* New York *magazine article she made public her sexual harassment claim against Harold Bloom. This essay was originally delivered as a commencement address at Scripps College in Claremont, California. Note that Wolf addresses her political subject with everyday examples of the double standard and other issues of how women are treated differently.*

Guillotine joke:

Once there was a revolution. Three revolutionaries were charged with treason—two men and a woman. The first revolutionary was taken to the guillotine. He was asked, "Do you want to die facing up or down?" "I'll face down." The headsman pulls the string—nothing happens. The crowd says, "It's a miracle! Set him

From *Next: Young American Writers on the New Generation,* edited by Eric Liu. Published by W. W. Norton & Company, Inc. Copyright © 1994 by Ric Liu. Selection copyright by Naomi Wolf.

free" The second man approaches the block and, given the same choice, he opts to face the ground. Again when the headsman pulls the string, nothing happens and the crowd cheers to set him free. The third revolutionary replies, "I'll face up." Headsman pulls string—nothing happens! She points upward and says, "I think I see what the problem is."

Even the best of revolutions can go awry when we begin to internalize the attitudes that we are fighting. During the past twenty years women have gained legal and reproductive rights as never before, have entered new jobs and professions. At the same time, anorexia and bulimia became epidemic; sexual assaults against women are at a record high, up 59 percent from last year; *Roe v. Wade* is about to be reconsidered in the Supreme Court; the weight of fashion models and Miss Americas plummeted, from 8 percent below the weight of the average American woman to 23 percent below. And the Blonde joke is enjoying a renaissance.

.You are graduating in the midst of a violent backlash against the advances women have made over the last twenty years. This backlash is taking many forms, from the sudden relevance of quotes from *The Exorcist* in Senate hearing rooms to beer commercials with the Swedish bikini team. What I want to give you today is a survival kit for the backlash into which you are about to graduate, a sort of five-step program to keep the dragons from taking up residence inside your own heads.

5First, let me tell you why it's so important for me to have been asked5 here today. My own graduation was the Commencement from Hell, an exercise in female disempowerment. I graduated eight years ago from Yale. The speaker was Dick Cavett, for little more reason than that he had been the college president's brother in an all-male secret society when they were both undergraduates. While the president was withdrawing college funds from South African investment, he was blind to the gender apartheid that he was endorsing on his own well-tended lawns.

Cavett took the microphone and seemed visibly to pale at the sight of two thousand female about-to-be Yale graduates. "When I was an undergraduate," he said, "there were no women here. The women went to Vassar. At Vassar," he said, "they had nude photographs taken of the women to check their posture in gym class. One year some of the photos were stolen, and they showed up for sale in New Haven's red-light district." His punch line? "The photos found no buyers."

I will never forget that moment. There were our parents and grandparents, many of whom had come long distances at great expense to be with us on our special day. There were we, silent in our black gowns, our tassels, our new shoes. We did not dare break the silence with boos or hisses, out of respect for our families who had given so much to make that day a success; and they in turn kept silent out of the same concern for us. Whether or not it was conscious, Cavett at that moment was using the beauty myth as it is often used in the backlash: whenever women get too close to masculine power, someone will draw critical attention to their bodies. Confronted with two thousand women who were about to become just as qualified as he himself was, his subtext was clear: you may be Elis, but you still wouldn't make pornography worth the buying.

That day, three thousand men were confirmed in the power of a powerful institution. But many of the two thousand women felt the shame of the powerless; the choking on silence, the complicity, the helplessness. We were orphaned from our institution at that moment—or rather, that moment laid bare the way in which the sons were truly sons all along, but the daughters were there on sufferance, intellectual and spiritual foster children whose membership in the family depended on self-effacement.

Commencement should be a rite of passage that makes you feel the opposite of how my graduation made me feel. My graduation did not celebrate in any way my wisdom and maturation as a woman; rather, it was a condescending pat on the head for having managed to "pass" for four years, in intellectual terms, as one of the boys.

So I want to give you the commencement talk I was denied. Since I'm only eight years older than you and still figuring things out myself, I don't feel comfortable using the second-person imperative in a way that would pretend that I have all the answers for your life. What I do when I say "you" is send a message back to my twenty-one-year-old self with the information I wish I had had then. As Gloria Steinem says, "we teach what we need to learn."

MESSAGE #1: The first message in your survival kit is to *cherish a new definition of what it means to "become a woman."* Today, you have ended your apprenticeship into the state of adult womanhood; today, you have "become women."

But that sounds terribly odd in ordinary usage, doesn't it? What is usually meant by the phrase "You're a real woman now"? Most connotations are biological: you "become a woman" when you menstruate for the first time, or when you lose your virginity, when you have a child.

Sometimes people say "a real woman" to suggest decorativeness—a real woman wears a DD-cup bra—or a state of matrimony: a man can make a "real" or "honest" woman out of someone by marrying her.

These merely endocrinological definitions of becoming a woman are very different from how we say boys become men. Someone "becomes a man" when he undertakes responsibility or successfully completes a dangerous quest. Let us make a new definition of "becoming a woman" that includes the fact that you, too, no less and in some ways more than your brothers and male friends graduating today, have not moved from childhood to adulthood by biological maturation alone but through your own successful completion of a struggle with new responsibilities—a difficult, ultimately solitary quest for the adult self.

But we have no archetypes for the questing young woman, her separation from home and family, her trials by fire. We lack words for how you become a woman through the chrysalis of education, the difficult passage from one book, one idea, to the next. My commencement pitted my scholarship and my gender against each other. We need a definition of "becoming a woman" in which a scholar learns womanhood and a woman learns scholarship, each term informing the other; Plato and Hegel, Djuna Barnes and particle physics, mediated to their own enrichment through the eyes and brain of the female body with its wisdoms and its gifts.

15 When I say that you have already showed courage in earning your 15 B.A.'s and passing through the forest, I am not talking about the demons of footnotes and poststructuralism. I'm talking about the extra lessons you had outside the classroom as well as in. Many of you graduate today in spite of the posttraumatic stress syndrome that follows acquaintance rape, which on campuses across America one-fourth of female undergraduates undergo. Many of you earned your credits while surviving on eight hundred calories a day, weak from ketosis and so faint from the anorexia that strikes one undergraduate woman in ten that it took every last ounce of your will to get your work in. Up to five times that number graduate today in spite of the crushing shame of bulimia, which consumes enormous energy and destroys self-esteem. You managed to stay focused on political theory and Greek while negotiating private lives through a minefield of new strains of VD, a 30 percent chlamydia rate among U.S. undergraduates, and the ascending shadow of HIV and AIDS. You had the force of imagination to believe that Emily Dickinson and Jane Austen still had something to say to you

while your airwaves flickered with ever more baroque and ingenious forms of glamorized violence against women.

Not to mention the more mundane trials of undergraduate life. You fell in love, fell in love with the wrong person, fell out of love, and survived love triangles, intrigues, betrayals, and jealousies. You took false starts in finding your life's work. Perhaps you questioned your religious assumptions, lost spiritual faith, found it again in forms that might alarm your grandparents, and lost it again to find it elsewhere anew. You lived through cliques, gossip, friends who borrowed your clothes and ruined them, dates from the Black Lagoon, money worries, second jobs, college loans, wardrobe angst, a Gulf war, earthquakes, and the way you break out magically just when you have an important job interview.

You made friends with people much richer or much poorer than your own families, and I trust that made you question how fairly this country distributes its wealth. You made friends with people of other racial and religious backgrounds and sexual affiliations than yourself, which I trust made you face the racism and homophobia that this culture embeds in all of our subconsciouses.

In earning your B.A.'s while fighting these battles so often labeled trivial, you have already proven that you are the triumphant survivors you will continue to have to be as you make your way through the backlash landscape outside this community. You have "become women," and as women, your commencement is not just a beginning but a confirmation of achievement. I applaud you.

MESSAGE #2 in your kit is the ultimate taboo subject for women. It makes grown women blush and fidget, and no, it's not sex. It's money. *Ask for money in your lives.* Expect it. Own it. Learn to use it. One of the most disempowering lessons we learn as little girls is the fear of money—that it's not nice, or feminine, to ensure that we are paid fairly for honest work. Meanwhile, women make fifty-nine cents for every male dollar and half of marriages end in divorce, at which point women's standard of living drops 43 percent. To cling to ignorance about money is to be gender illiterate.

Of course you must never choose a profession for material or status reasons, unless you want to guarantee your unhappiness. But, for God's sake, whatever field your heart chooses, get the highest, most specialized training in it you can and hold out hard for just compensation. You owe it to your daughters to fight a system that is happy to assign you to the class of highly competent, grossly underpaid women who run the show while others get the cash and the credit. Once you get your hands on every resource that is due to you, organize with other women for a better deal for the supports women need in the workplace—the parental leave and child care that European women take for granted, and that we need if we are to be what almost every man assumes he can be: both a parent and a worker.

Get the highest salary you can not out of selfish greed but so that you can tithe your income to women's political organizations, shelters, crisis lines, cultural events, and universities. Ten percent is a good guideline that I use myself. When you have equity, you have influence as sponsors, shareholders, trustees, and alumnae to force institutions into positive change. Male-dominated or racist institutions won't give up power if we are sweet and patient; the only language the status quo understands is money, votes, and public embarrassment. Use your clout to open opportunities to the women of all colors and classes who deserve the education and the training you had. As a woman, your B.A. and the income it represents don't belong to you alone, just as, in the Native American tradition, the earth doesn't belong to its present occupants alone. Your education was lent to you by women of the past who made it possible for you to have it; and it is your job to give some back to living women, as well as to your unborn daughters seven generations from now.

MESSAGE #3: *Never cook for or sleep with anyone who routinely puts you down.*

MESSAGE #4: *Honor your foremothers,* literal and metaphorical. Ask your mom or grandmother about her own life story, her own quest as she defines it. Read biographies of women of the past that you admire. Knowing how hard women worked because they believed in you will remind you, in dark moments, just how precious your freedom—and hence you—really are.

MESSAGE #5: *Give yourself the gift of speech;* become goddesses of disobedience. Sixty years ago Virginia Woolf wrote that we need to slay the Angel in the House, the self-sacrificing, compliant impulse in our own minds. It's still true. Across America, I meet young women who tell me stories of profound injustice: rape cover-ups on campus, blatant sexism in the classroom, discriminatory hiring and admission policies. When I suggest proven strategies to confront the injustice— like holding a press conference about campus crimes if the administration is unwilling to listen—they freeze at the suggestion, paralyzed into niceness. Their eyes take on a distant look, half longing, half petrified. If only! They laugh nervously. They would, but . . . people would get mad at them, they'd be called aggressive, the dean would hate their guts, the trustees might disapprove.

25   We are taught that the very worst thing we can do is cause conflict, even in the service of doing what is right. Antigone, you will remember, is imprisoned; Joan of Arc burns at the stake; and someone might call us unfeminine! Outrage, which we would not hesitate to express on behalf of a child, we are terrified of showing on behalf of ourselves, or other women.

This fear of not being liked is a big dragon in my own life. I saw the depths of my own paralysis by niceness when I wrote a book that caused controversy. *The Beauty Myth* argues that rigid ideals of beauty are part of the backlash against feminism, designed to lower women's self-esteem for a political purpose. While I meant every word I said, and while enormous positive changes followed, from heightened awareness about eating disorders to an FDA crackdown on breast implants, all of that would dwindle into insignificance when someone yelled at me— as plastic surgeons, for instance, often did on television. I would sob on my boyfriend's shoulder, People are mad at me! (Of course they were mad; a three-hundred-million-dollar industry was at stake.)

Halfway through the slings and arrows, I read something by African-American poet Audre Lorde that set me free to speak truth to power without blaming myself when power got a little annoyed.

Lorde was diagnosed with breast cancer. "I was going to die," she wrote, "sooner or later, whether or not I had ever *spoken* myself. My silences had not protected me. Your silence will not protect you. But for every real word spoken, I had made contact with other women while we examined words to fit a world in which we all believed . . . What are the words you do not yet have? What are the tyrannies you swallow day by day and attempt to make your own, until you will sicken and die of them, still in silence? We have been socialized to respect fear more than our own need for language."

So I began to ask, at every skirmish: "What's the worst that could happen to me if I tell this truth?" The fact is that the backlash greatly exaggerates the consequences of our speaking. Unlike women in other countries, our breaking silence is unlikely to land us in jail and tortured, or beaten with firehoses, or "disappeared," or run off the road at midnight. Our speaking out will make some people irritated, disrupt some dinner parties (and doubtless make them livelier), get us called names and ridiculed. And then our speaking out will permit other women to speak, and others, until laws are changed and lives are saved and the world is altered forever.

So I wish upon you the ability to distinguish between silencings. Some are real: if you will lose your livelihood or get the life beat out of you. You will respect the necessity of the circumstance at that moment and then organize like hell so you are not faced with it again. But then there are the other 90 percent, the petty, day-to-day silencings, like when you are being hassled by some drunken guests in a hotel and, rather than confronting them, the front desk tells you to lock yourself in your room. Or when your male classmates make sexist jokes. You know when you last swallowed your words.

Next time, ask yourself: What's the worst that will happen? So you might get called a bitch, or aggressive, or a slut, or the hostess will try to change the subject, or you might have to have a long talk with your male friends. Then, each time you are silenced, push yourself a little further than you think you dare to go. It will get easier and easier.

Then, once you are not immobilized with niceness, you know what? People *will* yell at you. They *will* interrupt, put you down, try to make you feel small, and suggest it's a personal problem. And the world won't end. And you will grow stronger by the day and find you have fallen in love with your own vision of the world, which you may never have known you had, because you were trying so hard not to know what you knew. And you will lose some friends and some lovers, and find you don't miss them; and new ones will find you. And you will still go dancing all night, still flirt and dress up and party, because as Emma Goldman said, "If I can't dance, it's not my revolution." And as time goes on you will know with surpassing certainty that there is only one thing more dangerous and frightening and harmful to your well-being than speaking your truth. And that is the certain psychic death of not speaking.

Questions on Meaning

1. Explain the point Wolf makes in the first paragraph. How do her examples support the argument that "revolutions can go awry when we begin to internalize the attitudes that we are fighting "?
2. What could Cavett have said about the joke he told to make it appealing rather than insulting to the audience?

Questions on Rhetorical Strategy and Style

1. Define the term *archetype* and explain Wolf's use of the term in her Message #1.
2. Does Wolf resort to stereotypes of women in the sentence, "You lived through cliques, gossip, friends who borrowed your clothes and ruined them, dates from the Black Lagoon . . . and the way you break out magically just when you have an important job interview"? Explain.

Writing Assignments

1. Rank Wolf's messages in order of their importance to you, and explain your ranking.
2. What causes women to be, or feel, silenced in important conversations where men are speaking? Does Wolf have the right idea about how to overcome silencing?
3. Write an essay on the verbal interactions between men and women. Begin with the problems Wolf describes and branch out by researching the work that Deborah Tannen has done with communication.

Size 6: The Western Women's Harem

Fatema Mernissi

Fatema Mernissi (1940–), a Moroccan feminist writer and sociologist, was born in Fez and studied at the Sorbonne in Paris. Her doctorate is from Brandeis University in the United States. She has published widely in the United States and won the 2003 Prince of Asturias Award for Letters (along with Susan Sontag). She now lives and works in Rabat, Morocco where she is a lecturer at the Mohammed V University of Rabat and a research scholar at the University Institute for Scientific Research. Her publications include Beyond the Veil: Male/Female Dynamics in Modern Muslim Society *(1975);* The Veil and the Male Elite: A Feminist Interpretation of Women's Rights in Islam *(1988);* Forgotten Queens of Islam *(1990);* Islam and Democracy: Fear of the Modern World *(1992); and* Scheherazade Goes West: Different Cultures, Different Harems *(2002).*

Moroccan women must hide their faces and live in a harem, but Western women have male domination inscribed into their flesh by the demands of a "size 6" world. The fashion industry is run by men who dictate that all women must look like adolescent girls. The author thanks God that she is not a Western woman but a Muslim who can eat what she wants.

It was during my unsuccessful attempt to buy a cotton skirt in an American department store that I was told my hips were too large to fit into a size 6. That distressing experience made me realize how the image of beauty in the West can hurt and humiliate a woman as much as the veil does when enforced by the state police in extremist nations such as Iran, Afghanistan, or Saudi Arabia. Yes, that day I stumbled onto one of the keys to the enigma of passive beauty in Western harem fantasies. The elegant saleslady in the American store looked at me without moving from her desk and said that she had no skirt my size. "In this whole big store, there is no skirt for me?" I said. "You are joking." I felt very suspicious and thought that she just might be too tired to help me. I could understand that. But then the saleswoman added a condescending judgment, which sounded to me like an imam's fatwa. It left no room for discussion:

"You are too big!" she said.

"I am too big compared to what?" I asked, looking at her intently, because I realized that I was facing a critical cultural gap here.

"Compared to a size 6," came the saleslady's reply.

Her voice had a clear-cut edge to it that is typical of those who enforce religious laws. "Size 4 and 6 are the norm," she went on, encouraged by my bewildered look. "Deviant sizes such as the one you need can be bought in special stores."

That was the first time that I had ever heard such nonsense about my size. In the Moroccan streets, men's flattering comments regarding my particularly generous hips have for decades led me to believe that the entire planet shared their convictions. It is true that with advancing age, I have been hearing fewer and fewer flattering comments when walking in the medina, and sometimes the silence around me in the bazaars is deafening. But since my face has never met with the local beauty standards, and I have often had to defend myself against remarks such as *zirafa* (giraffe), because of my long neck, I learned long ago not to rely too much on the outside world for my sense of self-worth. In fact, paradoxically, as I discovered when I went to Rabat as a student, it was the self-reliance that I had developed to protect myself against "beauty blackmail" that made me attractive to others. My male fellow students could not believe that I did not give a damn about what they thought about my body. "You know, my dear," I would say in response to one of them, "all I need to survive is bread, olives, and sardines. That you think my neck is too long is your problem, not mine."

In any case, when it comes to beauty and compliments, nothing is too serious or definite in the medina, where everything can be negotiated. But things seemed to be different in that American department store. In fact, I have to confess that I lost my usual self-confidence in that New York environment. Not that I am always sure of myself, but I don't walk around the Moroccan streets or down the university corridors wondering what people are thinking about me. Of course, when I hear a compliment, my ego expands like a cheese soufflé, but on the whole, I don't expect to hear much from others. Some mornings, I feel ugly because I am sick or tired; others, I feel wonderful because it is sunny out or I have written a good paragraph. But suddenly, in that peaceful American store that I had entered so triumphantly, as a sovereign consumer ready to spend money, I felt savagely attacked. My hips, until then the sign of a relaxed and unin-hibited maturity, were suddenly being condemned as a deformity. . . .

"And who says that everyone must be a size 6?" I joked to the saleslady that day, deliberately neglecting to mention size 4, which is the size of my skinny twelve-year-old niece.

At that point, the saleslady suddenly gave me an anxious look. "The norm is everywhere, my dear," she said. "It's all over, in the magazines, on television, in the ads. You can't escape it. There is Calvin Klein, Ralph Lauren, Gianni Versace, Giorgio Armani, Mario Valentino, Salvatore Ferragamo, Christian Dior, Yves Saint-Laurent, Christian Lacroix, and Jean-Paul Gaultier. Big department stores go by the norm." She paused and then concluded, "If they sold size 14 or 16, which is probably what you need, they would go bankrupt."

She stopped for a minute and then stared at me, intrigued. "Where on earth do you come from? I am sorry I can't help you. Really, I am." And she looked it too. She seemed, all of a sudden, interested, and brushed off another woman who was seeking her attention with a cutting, "Get someone else to help you, I'm busy." Only then did I notice that she was probably my age, in her late fifties. But unlike me, she had the thin body of an adolescent girl. Her knee-length, navy blue, Chanel dress had a white silk collar reminis-cent of the subdued elegance of aristocratic French Catholic school-girls at the turn of the century. A pearl-studded belt emphasized the slimness of her waist. With her meticulously styled short hair and sophisticated makeup, she looked half my age at first glance.

"I come from a country where there is no size for women's clothes," I told her. "I buy my own material and the neighborhood seamstress or craftsman makes me the silk or leather skirt I want. They just take my measurements each time I see them. Neither the seamstress nor I know exactly what size my new skirt is. We discover it together in the making. No one cares about my size in Morocco as long as I pay taxes on time. Actually, I don't know what my size is, to tell you the truth."

The saleswoman laughed merrily and said that I should advertise my country as a paradise for stressed working women. "You mean you don't watch your weight?" she inquired, with a tinge of disbelief in her voice. And then, after a brief moment of silence, she added in a lower register, as if talking to herself: "Many women working in highly paid fashion-related jobs could lose their positions if they didn't keep to a strict diet."

Her words sounded so simple, but the threat they implied was so cruel that I realized for the first time that maybe "size 6" is a more violent restriction imposed on women than is the Muslim veil. Quickly I said good-bye so as not to make any more demands on the saleslady's time or involve her in any more unwelcome, confidential exchanges about age-discriminating salary cuts. A surveillance camera was probably watching us both.

Yes, I thought as I wandered off, I have finally found the answer to my harem enigma. Unlike the Muslim man, who uses space to establish male domination by excluding women from the public arena, the Western man manipulates time and light. He declares that in order to be beautiful, a woman must look fourteen years old. If she dares to look fifty, or worse, sixty, she is beyond the pale. By putting the spotlight on the female child and framing her as the ideal of beauty, he condemns the mature woman to invisibility. In fact, the modern Western man enforces Immanuel Kant's nineteenth-century theories: To be beautiful, women have to appear childish and brainless. When a woman looks mature and self-assertive, or allows her hips to expand, she is condemned as ugly. Thus, the walls of the European harem separate youthful beauty from ugly maturity.

15 These Western attitudes, I thought, are even more dangerous and 15 cunning than the Muslim ones because the weapon used against women is time. Time is less visible, more fluid than space. The Western man uses

images and spotlights to freeze female beauty within an idealized childhood, and forces women to perceive aging—that normal unfolding of the years—as a shameful devaluation. "Here I am, transformed into a dinosaur," I caught myself saying aloud as I went up and down the rows of skirts in the store, hoping to prove the saleslady wrong—to no avail. This Western time-defined veil is even crazier than the space-defined one enforced by the ayatollahs.

The violence embodied in the Western harem is less visible than in the Eastern harem because aging is not attacked directly, but rather masked as an aesthetic choice. Yes, I suddenly felt not only very ugly but also quite useless in that store, where, if you had big hips, you were simply out of the picture. You drifted into the fringes of nothingness. By putting the spotlight on the prepubescent female, the Western man veils the older, more mature woman, wrapping her in shrouds of ugliness. This idea gives me the chills because it tattoos the invisible harem directly onto a woman's skin. Chinese foot-binding worked the same way: Men declared beautiful only those women who had small, childlike feet. Chinese men did not force women to bandage their feet to keep them from developing normally—all they did was to define the beauty ideal. In feudal China, a beautiful woman was the one who voluntarily sacrificed her right to unhindered physical movement by mutilating her own feet, and thereby proving that her main goal in life was to please men. Similarly, in the Western world, I was expected to shrink my hips into a size 6 if I wanted to find a decent skirt tailored for a beautiful woman. We Muslim women have only one month of fasting, Ramadan, but the poor Western woman who diets has to fast twelve months out of the year. "*Quelle horreur,*" I kept repeating to myself, while looking around at the American women shopping. All those my age looked like youthful teenagers. . . .

Now, at last, the mystery of my Western harem made sense. Framing youth as beauty and condemning maturity is the weapon used against women in the West just as limiting access to public space is the weapon used in the East. The objective remains identical in both cultures: to make women feel unwelcome, inadequate, and ugly. The power of the Western man resides in dictating what women should wear and how they should look. He controls the whole fashion industry, from cosmetics to underwear. The West, I realized, was the only part of the world where women's fashion is a man's business. In places like Morocco, where you design your own clothes and discuss them with craftsmen and -women, fashion is your own business. Not so in the West. . . .

But how does the system function? I wondered. Why do women accept it?

20 Of all the possible explanations, I like that of the French sociologist 20 Pierre Bourdieu the best. In his latest book, *La Domination Masculine,* he proposes something he calls *"la violence symbolique"*: "Symbolic violence is a form of power which is hammered directly on the body, and as if by magic, without any apparent physical constraint. But this magic operates only because it activates the codes pounded in the deepest layers of the body." Reading Bourdieu, I had the impression that I finally understood Western man's psyche better. The cosmetic and fashion industries are only the tip of the iceberg, he states, which is why women are so ready to adhere to their dictates. Something else is going on on a far deeper level. Otherwise, why would women belittle themselves spontaneously? Why, argues Bourdieu, would women make their lives more difficult, for example, by preferring men who are taller or older than they are? "The majority of French women wish to have a husband who is older and also, which seems consistent, bigger as far as size is concerned," writes Bourdieu. Caught in the enchanted submission characteristic of the symbolic violence inscribed in the mysterious layers of the flesh, women relinquish what he calls "les signes ordinaires de la hiérarchie sexuelle," the ordinary signs of sexual hierarchy, such as old age and a larger body. By so doing, explains Bourdieu, women spontaneously accept the subservient position. It is this spontaneity Bourdieu describes as magic enchantment.

Once I understood how this magic submission worked, I became very happy that the conservative ayatollahs do not know about it yet. If they did, they would readily switch to its sophisticated methods, because they are so much more effective. To deprive me of food is definitely the best way to paralyze my thinking capabilities. . . .

"I thank you, Allah, for sparing me the tyranny of the 'size 6 harem,'" I repeatedly said to myself while seated on the Paris-Casablanca flight, on my way back home at last. "I am so happy that the conservative male elite does not know about it. Imagine the fundamentalists switching from the veil to forcing women to fit size 6."

How can you stage a credible political demonstration and shout in the streets that your human rights have been violated when you cannot find the right skirt?

Questions on Meaning

1. Mernissi argues that the Western world represses women even more than does the Muslim world. What experience leads her to this conclusion, and what does she decide about her treatment in the department store?
2. Who defines fashion in the Western world, and who agrees to follow the rules of fashion? What effect does fashion have on women who are not pencil thin? How do women tend to feel about themselves in the Western world?
3. How do women get their clothes in the Muslim world? Why are the women indifferent to men's opinions about their body shapes?

Questions on Rhetorical Strategy and Style

1. The essay begins with a humiliating experience in which the narrator is told that she cannot buy clothes in a store because she is too fat. Why does this story seem so shocking? Or is it shocking? Are Westerners so accustomed to the rules of fashion that the event in the store seems natural? Why does the narrator compare religious law to the the saleswoman's pronouncements?
2. Mernissi discusses the Western fashion industry as if it were planned as an attack on women. Does this discussion at the center of her essay carry more force than if she had begun with the charge? Does her personal and intimate tone lead the reader to agree with her?
3. The essay ends with a humorous prayer that religious leaders will not discover the dictates of Western fashion because these dictates are far worse than being locked in a harem. What is so effective about ending on this personal note? Why is it so powerful to compare Western fashion to the thing in the Muslim world that women find so unbelievable and unbearable?

Writing Assignments

1. Spend some time in a public place such as the quad or dining hall of your school. Observe what women wear and note women's sizes. Write about the kinds of clothing women wear and how

much the women appear to weigh. Is Mernissi right according to your observations?

2. Gather some fashion magazines. Estimate the average weight of the models. Look carefully at the advertisements. Note the messages being sent about, for example, hair, eyes, waists, and feet. Write about the messages that the reader receives from the magazine.

3. We understand our own culture best by looking at another culture. Mernissi's technique of using a despised quality in Muslim culture to expose Western culture is a common approach in writing. Choose something in another culture that you do not understand or dislike. Then look carefully at your own culture to discover what parallels you can find. Write about the comparisons you discover.

What I've Learned from Men

Barbara Ehrenreich

Barbara Ehrenreich (1941–) was born in Montana and earned her Ph.D. from Rockefeller University. She is known as—and speaks of herself as—an independent and outspoken feminist, liberal, and democratic socialist. Most of her non-fiction writing could be classified as social criticism, including a number of books: The Hearts of Men *(1983),* Fear of Falling *(1989),* The Worst Years of Our Lives *(1990), and* Bait and Switch: The (Futile) Pursuit of the American Dream *(2005). Her* New York Times *best seller* Nickel and Dimed: on (Not) Getting By in America *(2001) exposed the reality of the working poor. Her novel,* Kipper's Game *was published in 1993. She is a regular essayist for* Time *and other magazines. "What I've Learned from Men" was first printed in* Ms. *magazine in 1985. Ehrenreich has the ability to make us laugh at things—including herself—as we see the deeper truths. Her use of detail to exemplify her ideas is particularly strong in this essay.*

1   For many years I believed that women had only one thing to learn from men: how to get the attention of a waiter by some means short of kicking over the table and shrieking. Never in my life have I gotten the attention of a waiter, unless it was an off-duty waiter whose car I'd accidentally scraped in a parking lot somewhere. Men, however, can summon a maître d' just by thinking the word "coffee," and this is a power women would be well-advised to study. What else would we possibly want to learn from them? How to interrupt someone in mid-sentence as if you were performing an act of conversational euthanasia? How to drop a pair of socks three feet from an open

From *Ms. Magazine*, 1985.

hamper and keep right on walking? How to make those weird guttural gargling sounds in the bathroom?

But now, at mid-life, I am willing to admit that there are some real and useful things to learn from men. Not from all men—in fact, we may have the most to learn from some of the men we like the least. This realization does not mean that my feminist principles have gone soft with age: what I think women could learn from men is how to get *tough*. After more than a decade of consciousness-raising, assertiveness training, and hand-to-hand combat in the battle of the sexes, we're still too ladylike. Let me try that again—we're just too *damn* ladylike.

Here is an example from my own experience, a story that I blush to recount. A few years ago, at an international conference held in an exotic and luxurious setting, a prestigious professor invited me to his room for what he said would be an intellectual discussion on matters of theoretical importance. So far, so good. I showed up promptly. But only minutes into the conversation—held in all-too-adjacent chairs— it emerged that he was interested in something more substantial than a meeting of minds. I was disgusted, but not enough to overcome 30-odd years of programming in ladylikeness. Every time his comments took a lecherous turn, I chattered distractingly; every time his hand found its way to my knee, I returned it as if it were something he had misplaced. This went on for an unconscionable period (as much as 20 minutes); then there was a minor scuffle, a dash for the door, and I was out—with nothing violated but my self-esteem. I, a full-grown feminist, conversant with such matters as rape crisis counseling and sexual harassment at the workplace, had behaved like a ninny—or, as I now understand it, like a lady.

The essence of ladylikeness is a persistent servility masked as "niceness." For example, we (women) tend to assume that it is our responsibility to keep everything "nice" even when the person we are with is rude, aggressive, or emotionally AWOL. (In the above example, I was so busy taking responsibility for preserving the veneer of "niceness" that I almost forgot to take responsibility for myself.) In conversations with men, we do almost all the work: sociologists have observed that in male-female social interactions it's the woman who throws out leading questions and verbal encouragements ("So how did you *feel* about that?" and so on) while the man, typically, says "Hmmmm." Wherever we go, we're perpetually smiling—the on-cue smile, like the now-out-moded curtsy, being one of our culture's little rituals of submission.

We're trained to feel embarrassed if we're praised, but if we see a criticism coming at us from miles down the road, we rush to acknowledge it. And when we're feeling aggressive or angry or resentful, we just tighten up our smiles or turn them into rueful little moues. In short, we spend a great deal of time acting like wimps.

5   For contrast, think of the macho stars we love to watch. Think, for example, of Mel Gibson facing down punk marauders in "The Road Warrior" . . . John Travolta swaggering his way through the early scenes of "Saturday Night Fever" . . . or Marlon Brando shrugging off the local law in "The Wild One." Would they simper their way through tight spots? Chatter aimlessly to keep the conversation going? Get all clutched up whenever they think they might—just might—have hurt someone's feelings? No, of course not, and therein, I think, lies their fascination for us.

The attraction of the "tough guy" is that he has—or at least seems to have—what most of us lack, and that is an aura of power and control. In an article, feminist psychiatrist Jean Baker Miller writes that "a woman's using self-determined power for herself is equivalent to selfishness [and] destructiveness"—an equation that makes us want to avoid even the appearance of power. Miller cites cases of women who get depressed just when they're on the verge of success—and of women who do succeed and then bury their achievement in self-deprecation. As an example, she describes one company's periodic meetings to recognize outstanding salespeople: when a woman is asked to say a few words about her achievement, she tends to say something like, "Well, I really don't know how it happened. I guess I was just lucky this time." In contrast, the men will cheerfully own up to the hard work, intelligence, and so on, to which they owe their success. By putting herself down, a woman avoids feeling brazenly powerful and potentially "selfish"; she also does the traditional lady's work of trying to make everyone else feel better ("She's not really so smart, after all, just lucky").

So we might as well get a little tougher. And a good place to start is by cutting back on the small acts of deference that we've been programmed to perform since girlhood. Like unnecessary smiling. For many women—waitresses, flight attendants, receptionists—smiling is an occupational requirement, but there's no reason for anyone to go around grinning when she's not being paid for it. I'd suggest that we save our off-duty smiles for when we truly feel like sharing them, and if you're not sure what to do with your face in the meantime, study Clint Eastwood's expressions—both of them.

Along the same lines, I think women should stop taking responsibility for every human interaction we engage in. In a social encounter with a woman, the average man can go 25 minutes saying nothing more than "You don't say?" "Izzat so?" and, of course, "Hmmmm." Why should we do all the work? By taking so much responsibility for making conversations go well, we act as if we had much more at stake in the encounter than the other party—and that gives him (or her) the power advantage. Every now and then, we deserve to get more out of a conversation than we put into it: I'd suggest not offering information you'd rather not share ("I'm really terrified that my sales plan won't work") and not, out of sheer politeness, soliciting information you don't really want ("Wherever did you get that lovely tie?"). There will be pauses, but they don't have to be awkward for *you.*

It is true that some, perhaps most, men will interpret any decrease in female deference as a deliberate act of hostility. Omit the free smiles and perky conversation-boosters and someone is bound to ask, "Well, what's come over *you* today?" For most of us, the first impulse is to stare at our feet and make vague references to a terminally ill aunt in Atlanta, but we should have as much right to be taciturn as the average (male) taxi driver. If you're taking a vacation from smiles and small talk and some fellow is moved to inquire about what's "bothering" you, just stare back levelly and say, the international debt crisis, the arms race, or the death of God.

There are all kinds of ways to toughen up—and potentially move up—at work, and I leave the details to the purveyors of assertiveness training. But Jean Baker Miller's study underscores a fundamental principle that anyone can master on her own. We can stop acting less capable than we actually are. For example, in the matter of taking credit when credit is due, there's a key difference between saying "I was just lucky" and saying "I had a plan and it worked." If you take the credit you deserve, you're letting people know that you were confident you'd succeed all along, and that you fully intend to do so again.

Finally, we may be able to learn something from men about what to do with anger. As a general rule, women get irritated: men get *mad.* We make tight little smiles of ladylike exasperation; they pound on desks and roar. I wouldn't recommend emulating the full basso profundo male tantrum, but women do need ways of expressing justified anger clearly, colorfully, and, when necessary, crudely. If you're not just irritated, but *pissed off,* it might help to say so.

I, for example, have rerun the scene with the prestigious professor many times in my mind. And in my mind, I play it like Bogart. I start by moving my chair over to where I can look the professor full in the face. I let him do the chattering, and when it becomes evident that he has nothing serious to say, I lean back and cross my arms, just to let him know that he's wasting my time. I do not smile, neither do I nod encouragement. Nor, of course, do I respond to his blandishments with apologetic shrugs and blushes. Then, at the first flicker of lechery, I stand up and announce coolly, "All right, I've had enough of this crap." Then I walk out—slowly, deliberately, confidently. Just like a man.

Or—now that I think of it—just like a woman.

Questions on Meaning

1. Ehrenreich equates "nice lady" with "ninny" and "wimp." Do you agree? Why or why not?
2. Describe in your own words what Ehrenreich means by "tough."

Questions on Rhetorical Strategy and Style

1. There seems to be a sort of contradiction in this essay: Ehrenreich describes men's behaviors in a negative manner but then says women should act in the same ways. Does she really want women to share what seem to be the faults of men? Or what other point is she making with this comparison?
2. Analyze how the essay's organizational pattern is based on a comparison and contrast of "nice ladies" and "tough guys."
3. Ehrenreich uses vivid examples throughout to illustrate her points about nice ladies and tough men. Pick out three or four of each, and describe why each is effective.
4. Comment on the role of humor in the essay, such as in the last four sentences of the opening paragraph. Do (or should) men and women equally find this funny? What is the role of humor throughout the essay?

Writing Assignments

1. Ehrenreich wrote this essay in 1985. Has much changed since then? Do you think it is more acceptable for women now to act more "like men" in the business and professional world? Talk with several professional women about their experiences. Do they feel like they must act like "nice ladies" in their business interactions? Are there ways they are consciously getting "tougher"?
2. Asks several men about their perceptions of differences between men and women in the business and professional world. Although it is "politically correct" for men to say they believe in full equality with women in every way, do you see any signs that men may still have a double standard?
3. Ehrenreich uses narration to tell the story of her encounter with the lecherous professor, concluding with her thoughts of what she should have done. This story allows her to reflect on her own actions and recognize a better course of action. We all have had experiences in which we later realize we should have acted in a

different manner. Think of such an experience you have had yourself, and write a narrative essay that both describes the experience
itself and analyzes its meaning for you at the time and later.

Ad Analysis

Advertising's Fifteen Basic Appeals

Jib Fowles

Jib Fowles (1940–) was born in Hartford, Connecticut and attended Wesleyan University, Columbia University, and New York University, where he received a Ph.D. in 1974. Currently he is professor of communication at the University of Houston. A Fulbright Scholar, he has pub-lished extensively on the subject of mass culture, advertis-ing, media, and their effects on the public. His most recent works include Starstruck: Celebrity Performers and the American Public *(1992);* Why Viewers Watch: A Reap-praisal of Television's Effects *(1992);* Advertising and Popular Culture *(1996); and* The Case for Television Violence *(1999). The following selection is excerpted from the article "Mass Advertising as Social Forecast."*

Emotional Appeals

1   The nature of effective advertisements was recognized full well by the late media philosopher Marshall McLuhan. In his *Understanding Media,* the first sentence of the section on advertising reads, "The continuous pressure is to create ads more and more in the image of audience motives and desires."

By giving form to people's deep-lying desires, and picturing states of being that individuals privately yearn for, advertisers have the best chance of arresting attention and affecting communication. And that is the immediate goal of advertising: to tug at our psychological shirtsleeves and slow us down long enough for a word or two about whatever is being sold. We glance at a picture of a solitary rancher at work, and "Marlboro" slips into our minds.

Advertisers (I'm using the term as a shorthand for both the products' manufacturers, who bring the ambition and money to the process, and the advertising agencies, who supply the know-how) are ever more compelled to invoke consumers' drives and longings; this is the "continuous pressure" McLuhan refers to. Over the past century, the American marketplace has grown increasingly congested as more and more products have entered into the frenzied competition after the public's dollars. The economies of other nations are quieter than ours since the volume of goods being hawked does not so greatly exceed demand. In some economies, consumer wares are scarce enough that no advertising at all is necessary. But in the United States, we go to the other extreme. In order to stay in business, an advertiser must strive to cut through the considerable commercial hub-bub by any means available—including the emotional appeals that some observers have held to be abhorrent and underhanded.

The use of subconscious appeals is a comment not only on conditions among sellers. As time has gone by, buyers have become stoutly resistant to advertisements. We live in a blizzard of these messages and have learned to turn up our collars and ward off most of them. A study done a few years ago at Harvard University's Graduate School of Business Administration ventured that the average American is exposed to some 500 ads daily from television, newspapers, magazines, radio, billboards, direct mail, and so on. If for no other reason than to preserve one's sanity, a filter must be developed in every mind to lower the number of ads a person is actually aware of—a number this particular study estimated at about seventy-five ads per day. (Of these, only twelve typically produced a reaction—nine positive and three negative, on the average.) To be among the few messages that do manage to gain access to minds, advertisers must be strategic, perhaps even a little underhanded at times.

5   There are assumptions about personality underlying advertisers'   5
efforts to communicate via emotional appeals, and while these assumptions have stood the test of time, they still deserve to be aired. Human beings, it is presumed, walk around with a variety of unfulfilled urges and motives swirling in the bottom half of their minds. Lusts, ambitions, tendernesses, vulnerabilities—they are constantly bubbling up, seeking resolution. These mental forces energize

people, but they are too crude and irregular to be given excessive play in the real world. They must be capped with the competent, sensible behavior that permits individuals to get along well in society. However, this upper layer of mental activity, shot through with caution and rationality, is not receptive to advertising's pitches. Advertisers want to circumvent this shell of consciousness if they can, and latch on to one of the lurching, subconscious drives.

In effect, advertisers over the years have blindly felt their way around the underside of the American psyche, and by trial and error have discovered the softest points of entree, the places where their messages have the greatest likelihood of getting by consumers' defenses. As McLuhan says elsewhere, "Gouging away at the surface of public sales resistance, the ad men are constantly breaking through into the *Alice in Wonderland* territory behind the looking glass, which is the world of subrational impulses and appetites."

An advertisement communicates by making use of a specially selected image (of a supine female, say, or a curly-haired child, or a celebrity) which is designed to stimulate "subrational impulses and desires" even when they are at ebb, even if they are unacknowledged by their possessor. Some few ads have their emotional appeal in the text, but for the greater number by far the appeal is contained in the artwork. This makes sense, since visual communication better suits more primal levels of the brain. If the viewer of an advertisement actually has the importuned motive, and if the appeal is sufficiently well fashioned to call it up, then the person can be hooked. The product in the ad may then appear to take on the semblance of gratification for the summoned motive. Many ads seem to be saying, "If you have this need, then this product will help satisfy it." It is a primitive equation, but not an ineffective one for selling.

Thus, most advertisements appearing in national media can be understood as having two orders of content. The first is the appeal to deep-running drives in the minds of consumers. The second is information regarding the good[s] or service being sold: its name, its manufacturer, its picture, its packaging, its objective attributes, its functions. For example, the reader of a brassiere advertisement sees a partially undraped but blandly unperturbed woman standing in an otherwise commonplace public setting, and may experience certain sensations; the reader also sees the name "Maidenform," a particular brassiere style, and, in tiny print, words about the material, colors, price. Or, the viewer of a television commercial sees a demonstration with four small boxes labeled 650, 650, 650, and 800; something in the viewer's mind catches hold of this, as trivial as thoughtful consideration might reveal it to be. The viewer is also exposed to the name "Anacin," its bottle, and its purpose.

Sometimes there is an apparently logical link between an ad's emotional appeal and its product information. It does not violate common sense that Cadillac automobiles be photographed at country clubs, or that Japan Air Lines be associated with Orientalia. But there is no real need for the linkage to have a bit of reason behind it. Is there anything inherent to the connection between Salem cigarettes and mountains, Coke and a smile, Miller Beer and comradeship? The link being forged in minds between product and appeal is a pre-logical one.

10   People involved in the advertising industry do not necessarily talk   10
in the terms being used here. They are stationed at the sending end of this communications channel, and may think they are up to any number of things—Unique Selling Propositions, explosive copywriting, the optimal use of demographics or psychographics, ideal media buys, high recall ratings, or whatever. But when attention shifts to the receiving end of the channel, and focuses on the instant of reception, then commentary becomes much more elemental: an advertising message contains something primary and primitive, an emotional appeal, that in effect is the thin end of the wedge, trying to find its way into a mind. Should this occur, the product information comes along behind.

When enough advertisements are examined in this light, it becomes clear that the emotional appeals fall into several distinguishable categories, and that every ad is a variation on one of a limited number of basic appeals. While there may be several ways of classifying these appeals, one particular list of fifteen has proven to be especially valuable.

Advertisements can appeal to:
1. The need for sex
2. The need for affiliation
3. The need to nurture
4. The need for guidance
5. The need to aggress

6. The need to achieve
7. The need to dominate
8. The need for prominence
9. The need for attention
10. The need for autonomy
11. The need to escape
12. The need to feel safe
13. The need for aesthetic sensations
14. The need to satisfy curiosity
15. Physiological needs: food, drink, sleep, etc.

Murray's List

Where does this list of advertising's fifteen basic appeals come from? Several years ago, I was involved in a research project which was to have as one segment an objective analysis of the changing appeals made in post-World War II American advertising. A sample of magazine ads would have their appeals coded into the categories of psychological needs they seemed aimed at. For this content analysis to happen, a complete roster of human motives would have to be found.

The first thing that came to mind was Abraham Maslow's famous four-part hierarchy of needs. But the briefest look at the range of appeals made in advertising was enough to reveal that they are more varied, and more profane, than Maslow had cared to account for. The search led on to the work of psychologist Henry A. Murray, who together with his colleagues at the Harvard Psychological Clinic has constructed a full taxonomy of needs. As described in *Explorations in Personality*, Murray's team had conducted a lengthy series of in-depth interviews with a number of subjects in order to derive from scratch what they felt to be the essential variables of personality. Forty-four variables were distinguished by the Harvard group, of which twenty were motives. The need for achievement ("to overcome obstacles and obtain a high standard") was one, for instance; the need to defer was another; the need to aggress was a third; and so forth.

Murray's list had served as the groundwork for a number of subsequent projects. Perhaps the best-known of these was David C. McClelland's extensive study of the need for achievement, reported in his *The Achieving Society*. In the process of demonstrating that a people's high need for achievement is predictive of later economic growth, McClelland coded achievement imagery and references out of a nation's folklore, songs, legends, and children's tales.

15   Following McClelland, I too wanted to cull the motivational appeals   15 from a culture's imaginative product—in this case, advertising. To develop categories expressly for this purpose, I took Murray's twenty motives and added to them others he had mentioned in passing in *Explorations in Personality* but not included on the final list. The extended list was tried out on a sample of advertisements, and motives which never seemed to be invoked were dropped. I ended up with eighteen of Murrays' motives, into which 770 print ads were coded. The resulting distribution is included in the 1976 book *Mass Advertising as Social Forecast.*

Since that time, the list of appeals has undergone refinements as a result of using it to analyze television commercials. A few more adjustments stemmed from the efforts of students in my advertising classes to decode appeals; tens of term papers surveying thousands of advertisements have caused some inconsistencies in the list to be hammered out. Fundamentally, though, the list remains the creation of Henry Murray. In developing a comprehensive, parsimonious inventory of human motives, he pinpointed the subsurface mental forces that are the least quiescent and most susceptible to advertising's entreaties.

Fifteen Appeals

1. Need for Sex.   Let's start with sex, because this is the appeal which seems to pop up first whenever the topic of advertising is raised. Whole books have been written about this one alone, to find a large audience of mildly titillated readers. Lately, due to campaigns to sell blue jeans, concern with sex in ads has redoubled.

The fascinating thing is not how much sex there is in advertising, but how little. Contrary to impressions, unambiguous sex is rare in these messages. Some of this surprising observation may be a matter of definition: the Jordache ads with the lithe, blouse-less female astride a similarly clad male is clearly an appeal to the audience's sexual drives, but the same cannot be said about Brooke Shields[1] in the Calvin Klein commercials. Directed at young women and their credit-card carrying mothers, the image of Miss Shields instead invokes the need to be looked at. Buy Calvins and you'll be the center of much attention, just as Brooke is, the ads imply; they do not primarily inveigle their target audience's need for sexual intercourse.

In the content analysis reported in *Mass Advertising as Social Forecast* only two percent of ads were found to pander to this motive. Even *Playboy* ads shy away from sexual appeals: a recent issue contained eighty-three full-page ads, and just four of them (or less than five percent) could be said to have sex on their minds.

20   The reason this appeal is so little used is that it is too blaring and   20 tends to obliterate the product information. Nudity in advertising has the effect of reducing brand recall. The people who do remember the product may do so because they have been made indignant by the ad; this is not the response most advertisers seek.

To the extent that sexual imagery is used, it conventionally works better on men than women; typically a female figure is offered up to the male reader. A Black Velvet liquor advertisement displays an attractive woman wearing a tight black outfit, recumbent under the legend, "Feel the Velvet." The figure does not have to be horizontal, however, for the appeal to be present as National Airlines revealed in its "Fly me" campaign. Indeed, there does not even have to be a female in the ad; "Flick my Bic"[2] was sufficient to convey the idea to many.

As a rule, though, advertisers have found sex to be a tricky appeal, to be used sparingly. Less controversial and equally fetching are the appeals to our need for affectionate human contact.

2. Need for Affiliation.   American mythology upholds autonomous individuals, and social statistics suggest that people are ever more going it alone in their lives, yet the high frequency of affiliative appeals in ads belies this. Or maybe it does not: maybe all the images of companionship are compensation for what Americans privately lack. In any case, the need to associate with others is widely invoked in advertising and is probably the most prevalent appeal. All sorts of goods and services are sold by linking them to our unfulfilled desires to be in good company.

According to Henry Murray, the need for affiliation consists of desires "to draw near and enjoyably cooperate or reciprocate with another; to please and win affection of another; to adhere and remain loyal to a friend." The manifestations of this motive can be segmented into several different types of affiliation, beginning with romance.

25   Courtship may be swifter nowadays, but the desire for pair-bonding   25 is far from satiated. Ads reaching for this need commonly depict a youngish male and female engrossed in each other. The head of the male is usually higher than the female's, even at this late date; she may

be sitting or leaning while he is standing. They are not touching in the Smirnoff vodka ads, but obviously there is an intimacy, sometimes frolicsome, between them. The couple does touch for Martell Cognac when "The moment was Martell." For Wind Song perfume they have touched, and "Your Wind Song stays on his mind."

Depending on the audience, the pair does not absolutely have to be young—just together. He gives her a DeBeers diamond, and there is a tear in her laugh lines. She takes Geritol[3] and preserves herself for him. And numbers of consumers, wanting affection too, follow suit.

Warm family feelings are fanned in ads when another generation is added to the pair. Hallmark Cards brings grandparents into the picture, and Johnson and Johnson Baby Powder has Dad, Mom, and baby, all fresh from the bath, encircled in arms and emblazoned with "Share the Feeling." A talc has been fused to familial love.

Friendship is yet another form of affiliation pursued by advertisers. Two women confide and drink Maxwell House coffee together; two men walk through the woods smoking Salem cigarettes. Miller Beer promises that afternoon "Miller Time" will be staffed with three or four good buddies. Drink Dr. Pepper, as Mickey Rooney[4] is coaxed to do, and join in with all the other Peppers. Coca-Cola does not even need to portray the friendliness; it has reduced this appeal to "a Coke and a smile."

The warmth can be toned down and disguised, but it is the same affiliative need that is being fished for. The blonde has a direct gaze and her friends are firm businessmen in appearance, but with a glass of Old Bushmill you can sit down and fit right in. Or, for something more upbeat, sing along with the Pontiac choirboys.

30 As well as presenting positive images, advertisers can play to 30 the need for affiliation in negative ways, by invoking the fear of rejection. If we don't use Scope, we'll have the "Ugh! Morning Breath" that causes the male and female models to avert their faces. Unless we apply Ultra Brite or Close-Up to our teeth, it's good-bye romance. Our family will be cursed with "House-a-tosis" if we don't take care. Without Dr. Scholl's antiperspirant foot spray, the bowling team will keel over. There go all the guests when the supply of Dorito's nacho cheese chips is exhausted. Still more rejection if our shirts have ring-around-the-collar, if our car needs to be Midasized. But make a few purchases, and we are back in the bosom of human contact.

As self-directed as Americans pretend to be, in the last analysis we remain social animals, hungering for the positive, endorsing feelings that only those around us can supply. Advertisers respond, urging us to "Reach out and touch someone," in the hopes our monthly [phone] bills will rise.

3. Need to Nurture. Akin to affiliative needs is the need to take care of small, defenseless creatures—children and pets, largely. Reciprocity is of less consequence here, though; it is the giving that counts. Murray uses synonyms like "to feed, help, support, console, protect, comfort, nurse, heal." A strong need it is, woven deep into our genetic fabric, for if it did not exist we could not successfully raise up our replacements. When advertisers put forth the image of something diminutive and furry, something that elicits the word "cute" or "precious," then they are trying to trigger this motive. We listen to the childish voice singing the Oscar Mayer weiner song, and our next hot-dog purchase is prescribed. Aren't those darling kittens something, and how did this Meow Mix get into our shopping cart?

This pitch is often directed at women, as Mother Nature's chief nurturers. "Make me some Kraft macaroni and cheese, please," says the elfin preschooler just in from the snowstorm, and mothers' hearts go out, and Kraft's sales go up. "We're cold, wet, and hungry," whine the husband and kids, and the little woman gets the Manwiches ready. A facsimile of this need can be hit without children or pets: the husband is ill and sleepless in the television commercial, and the wife grudgingly fetches the NyQuil.

But it is not women alone who can be touched by this appeal. The father nurses his son Eddie through adolescence while the John Deere lawn tractor survives the years. Another father counts pennies with his young son as the subject of New York Life Insurance comes up. And all over America are businessmen who don't know why they dial Qantas Airlines[5] when they have to take a trans-Pacific trip; the koala bear knows.

4. Need for Guidance. The opposite of the need to nurture is the need to be nurtured: to be protected, shielded, guided. We may be loath to admit it, but the child lingers on inside every adult—and a good thing it does, or we would not be instructable in our advancing years. Who wants a nation of nothing but flinty personalities?

Parent-like figures can successfully call up this need. Robert Young[6] recommends Sanka coffee, and since we have experienced him for twenty-five years as television father and doctor, we take his word for it. Florence Henderson[7] as the expert mom knows a lot about the advantages of Wesson oil.

The parent-ness of the spokesperson need not be so salient; sometimes pure authoritativeness is better. When Orson Welles[8] scowls and intones, "Paul Masson will sell no wine before its time," we may not know exactly what he means, but we still take direction from him. There is little maternal about Brenda Vaccaro[9] when she speaks up for Tampax, but there is a certainty to her that many accept.

A celebrity is not a necessity in making a pitch to the need for guidance, since a fantasy figure can serve just as well. People accede to the Green Giant, or Betty Crocker, or Mr. Goodwrench.[10] Some advertisers can get by with no figure at all: "When E. F. Hutton[11] talks, people listen."

Often it is tradition or custom that advertisers point to and consumers take guidance from. Bits and pieces of American history are used to sell whiskeys like Old Crow, Southern Comfort, Jack Daniel's. We conform to traditional male/female roles and age-old social norms when we purchase Barclay cigarettes, which informs us "The pleasure is back."

40 The product itself, if it has been around for a long time, can 40 constitute a tradition. All those old labels in the ad for Morton salt convince us that we should continue to buy it. Kool-Aid says "You loved it as a kid. You trust it as a mother," hoping to get yet more consumers to go along.

Even when the product has no history at all, our need to conform to tradition and to be guided are strong enough that they can be invoked through bogus nostalgia and older actors. Country-Time lemonade sells because consumers want to believe it has a past they can defer to.

So far the needs and the ways they can be invoked which have been looked at are largely warm and affiliative; they stand in contrast to the next set of needs, which are much more egoistic and assertive.

5. Need to Aggress. The pressures of the real world create strong retaliatory feelings in every functioning human being. Since these impulses can come forth as bursts of anger and violence, their display is normally tabooed. Existing as harbored energy, aggressive drives present a large, tempting target for advertisers. It is not a target to be aimed at thoughtlessly, though, for few manufacturers want their products associated with destructive motives. There is always the danger that, as in the case of sex, if the appeal is too blatant, public opinion will turn against what is being sold.

Jack-in-the-Box sought to abruptly alter its marketing by going after older customers and forgetting the younger ones. Their television commercials had a seventy-ish lady command, "Waste him," and the Jack-in-the-Box clown exploded before our eyes. So did public reaction until the commercials were toned down. Print ads for Club cocktails carried the faces of octogenarians under the headline, "Hit me with a Club"; response was contrary enough to bring the campaign to a stop.

Better disguised aggressive appeals are less likely to backfire: Triumph cigarettes has models making a lewd gesture with their uplifted cigarettes, but the individuals are often laughing and usually in close company of others. When Exxon said, "There's a Tiger in your tank," the implausibility of it concealed the invocation of aggressive feelings.

Depicted arguments are a common way for advertisers to tap the audience's needs to aggress. Don Rickles[12] and Lynda Carter[13] trade gibes, and consumers take sides as the name of Seven-Up is stitched on minds. The Parkay [margarine] tub has a difference of opinion with the user; who can forget it, or who (or what) got the last word in?

6. Need to Achieve. This is the drive that energizes people, causing them to strive in their lives and careers. According to Murray, the need for achievement is signalled by the desires "to accomplish something difficult. To overcome obstacles and attain a high standard. To excel one's self. To rival and surpass others." A prominent American trait, it is one that advertisers like to hook on to because it identifies their product with winning and success.

The Cutty Sark ad does not disclose that Ted Turner failed at his latest attempt at yachting's America Cup; here he is represented as a champion on the water as well as off in his television enterprises. If we drink this whiskey, we will be victorious alongside Turner. We can also succeed with O. J. Simpson[14] by renting Hertz cars, or with Reggie Jackson[15] by bringing home some Panasonic equipment. Cathy Rigby[16] and Stayfree maxipads will put people out front.

Sports heroes are the most convenient means to snare consumers' needs to achieve, but they are not the only one. Role models can be established, ones which invite emulation, as with the profiles put forth by Dewar's scotch. Successful, tweedy individuals relate they have "graduated to the flavor of Myer's rum." Or the advertiser can establish a prize: two neighbors play one-on-one basketball for a Michelob beer in a television commercial, while in a print ad a bottle of Johnnie Walker Black Label has been gilded like a trophy.

50 Any product that advertises itself in superlatives—the best, the first, the finest—is trying to make contact with our needs to succeed. For many consumers, sales and bargains belong in this category of appeals, too; the person who manages to buy something at fifty percent off is seizing an opportunity and coming out ahead of others.

7. Need to Dominate. This fundamental need is the craving to be powerful—perhaps omnipotent, as in the Xerox ad where Brother Dominic exhibits heavenly powers and creates miraculous copies. Most of us will settle for being just a regular potentate, though. We drink Budweiser because it is the King of Beers, and here comes the powerful Clydesdales to prove it. A taste of Wolfschmidt vodka and "The spirit of the Czar lives on."

The need to dominate and control one's environment is often thought of as being masculine, but as close students of human nature advertisers know, it is not so circumscribed. Women's aspirations for control are suggested in the campaign theme, "I like my men in English Leather, or nothing at all." The females in the Chanel No. 19 ads are "outspoken" and wrestle their men around.

Male and female, what we long for is clout; what we get in its place is Mastercard.

8. Need for Prominence. Here comes the need to be admired and respected, to enjoy prestige and high social status. These times, it appears, are not so egalitarian after all. Many ads picture the trappings of high position; the Oldsmobile stands before a manorial doorway, the Volvo is parked beside a steeplechase. A book-lined study is the setting for Dewar's 12, and Lenox China is displayed in a dining room chock full of antiques.

55 Beefeater gin represents itself as "The Crown Jewel of England" and uses no illustrations of jewels or things British, for the words are sufficient indicators of distinction. Buy that gin and you will rise up the prestige hierarchy, or achieve the same effect on yourself with Seagram's 7 Crown, which ambiguously describes itself as "classy."

Being respected does not have to entail the usual accoutrements of wealth: "Do you know who I am?" the commercials ask, and we learn that the prominent person is not so prominent without his American Express card.

9. Need for Attention. The previous need involved being *looked up to,* while this is the need to be *looked at.* The desire to exhibit ourselves in such a way as to make others look at us is a primitive, insuppressible instinct. The clothing and cosmetic industries exist just to serve this need, and this is the way they pitch their wares. Some of this effort is aimed at males, as the ads for Hathaway shirts and Jockey underclothes. But the greater bulk of such appeals is targeted singlemindedly at women.

To come back to Brooke Shields: this is where she fits into American marketing. If I buy Calvin Klein jeans, consumers infer, I'll be the object of fascination. The desire for exhibition has been most strikingly played to in a print campaign of many years' duration, that of Maidenform lingerie. The woman exposes herself, and sales surge. "Gentlemen prefer Hanes" the ads dissemble, and women who want eyes upon them know what they should do. Peggy Fleming[17] flutters her legs for L'eggs, encouraging females who want to be the star in their own lives to purchase this product.

The same appeal works for cosmetics and lotions. For years, the little girl with the exposed backside sold gobs of Coppertone, but now the company has picked up the pace a little: as a female, you are supposed to "Flash 'em a Coppertone tan." Food can be sold the same way, especially to the diet-conscious; Angie Dickinson poses for California avocados and says, "Would this body lie to you?" Our eyes are too fixed on her for us to think to ask if she got that way by eating mounds of guacomole.

10. Need for Autonomy. There are several ways to sell credit card services, as has been noted: Mastercard appeals to the need to dominate, and American Express to the need for prominence. When Visa claims, "You can have it the way you want it," yet another primary motive is being beckoned forward—the need to endorse the self. The focus here is upon the independence and integrity of the individual; this need is the antithesis of the need for guidance and is unlike any of the social needs. "If running with the herd isn't your style, try ours," says Rotan-Mosle, and many Americans feel they have finally found the right brokerage firm.

The photo is of a red-coated Mountie on his horse, posed on a snow-covered ledge; the copy reads, "Windsor—One Canadian stands alone." This epitome of the solitary and proud individual may work best with male customers as may Winston's man in the red cap. But one-figure advertisements also strike the strong need for autonomy among American women. As Shelly Hack[18] strides for Charlie perfume, females respond to her obvious pride and flair; she is her own person. The Virginia Slims tale is of people who have come a long way from subservience to independence. Cachet perfume feels it does not need a solo figure to work this appeal, and uses three different faces in its ads; it insists though, "It's different on every woman who wears it."

Like many psychological needs, this one can also be appealed to in a negative fashion, by invoking the loss of independence or self-regard. Guilt and regrets can be stimulated: "Gee, I could have had a V-8." Next time, get one and be good to yourself.

11. Need to Escape. An appeal to the need for autonomy often co-occurs with one for the need to escape, since the desire to duck out of our social oblications, to seek rest or adventure, frequently takes the form of one-person flight. The dashing image of a pilot, in fact, is a standard way of quickening this need to get away from it all.

Freedom is the pitch here, the freedom that every individual yearns for whenever life becomes too oppressive. Many advertisers like appealing to the need for escape because the sensation of pleasure often accompanies escape, and what nicer emotional nimbus could there be for a product? "You deserve a break today," says McDonald's, and Stouffer's frozen foods chime in, "Set yourself free."

65 For decades men have imaginatively bonded themselves to the 65 Marlboro cowboy who dwells untarnished and unencumbered in Marlboro Country some distance from modern life; smokers' aching needs for autonomy and escape are personified by that cowpoke. Many women can identify with the lady ambling through the woods behind the words, "Benson and Hedges and mornings and me."

But escape does not have to be solitary. Other Benson and Hedges ads, part of the same campaign, contain two strolling figures. In Salem cigarette advertisements, it can be several people who escape together into the mountaintops. A commercial for Levi's pictured a cloudbank above a city through which ran a whole chain of young people.

There are varieties of escape, some wistful like the Boeing "Someday" campaign of dream vacations, some kinetic like the play and parties in soft drink ads. But in every instance, the consumer exposed to the advertisement is invited to momentarily depart his everyday life for a more carefree experience, preferably with the product in hand.

12. Need to Feel Safe. Nobody in their right mind wants to be intimidated, menaced, battered, poisoned. We naturally want to do whatever it takes to stave off threats to our well-being, and to our families'. It is the instinct of self-preservation that makes us responsive to the ad of the St. Bernard with the keg of Chivas Regal. We pay attention to the stern talk of Karl Malden[19] and the plight of the vacationing couples who have lost all their funds in the American Express travelers cheques commercials. We want the omnipresent stag from Hartford Insurance to watch over us too.

In the interest of keeping failure and calamity from our lives, we like to see the durability of products demonstrated. Can we ever forget that Timex takes a licking and keeps on ticking? When the American Tourister suitcase bounces all over the highway and the egg inside doesn't break, the need to feel safe has been adroitly plucked.

We take precautions to diminish future threats. We buy Volkswagen Rabbits for the extraordinary mileage, and MONY insurance policies to avoid the tragedies depicted in their black-and-white ads of widows and orphans.

We are careful about our health. We consume Mazola margarine because it has "corn goodness" backed by the natural food traditions of the American Indians. In the medicine cabinet is Alka-Seltzer, the "home remedy"; having it, we are snug in our little cottage.

We want to be safe and secure; buy these products, advertisers are saying, and you'll be safer than you are without them.

13. Need for Aesthetic Sensations. There is an undeniable aesthetic component to virtually every ad run in the national media: the photography or filming or drawing is near-perfect, the type style is well chosen, the layout could scarcely be improved upon. Advertisers know there is little chance of good communication occurring if an ad is not visually pleasing. Consumers may not be aware of the extent of their own sensitivity to artwork, but it is undeniably large.

Sometimes the aesthetic element is expanded and made into an ad's primary appeal. Charles Jordan shoes may or may not appear in the accompanying avant-grade photographs; Kohler plumbing fixtures catch attention through the high style of their desert settings. Beneath the slightly out of focus photograph, languid and sensuous in tone, General Electric feels called upon to explain, "This is an ad for the hair dryer."

This appeal is not limited to female consumers: J&B scotch says "It whispers" and shows a bucolic scene of lake and castle.

14. Need to Satisfy Curiosity. It may seem odd to list a need for information among basic motives, but this need can be as primal and compelling as any of the others. Human beings are curious by nature, interested in the world around them, and intrigued by tidbits of knowledge and new developments Trivia, percentages, observations counter to conventional wisdom—these items all help sell products. Any advertisement in a question-and-answer format is strumming this need.

A dog groomer has a question about long distance rates, and Bell Telephone has a chart with all the figures. An ad for Porsche 911 is replete with diagrams and schematics, numbers and arrows. Lo and behold, Anacin pills have 150 more milligrams than its competitors; should we wonder if this is better of worse for us?

15. Physiological Needs. To the extent that sex is solely a biological need, we are now coming around full circle, back toward the start of the list. In this final category are clustered appeals to sleeping, eating, drinking. The art of photographing food and drink is so advanced, sometimes these temptations are wondrously caught in the camera's lens: the crab meat in the Red Lobster restaurant ads can start us salivating, the Quarterpounder can almost be smelled, the liquor in the glass glows invitingly. Imbibe, these ads scream.

Styles

Some common ingredients of advertisements were not singled out for separate mention in the list of fifteen because they are not appeals in and of themselves. They are stylistic features, influencing the way a basic appeal is presented. The use of humor is one, and the use of celebrities is another. A third is time imagery, past and future, which goes to several purposes.

For all of its employment in advertising, humor can be treacherous, because it can get out of hand and smother the product information. Supposedly, this is what Alka-Seltzer discovered with its comic commercials of the late sixties; "I can't believe I ate the whole thing," the sad-faced husband lamented, and the audience cackled so much it forgot the antacid. Or, did not take it seriously.

But used carefully, humor can punctuate some of the softer appeals and soften some of the harsher ones. When Emma says to the Fruit-of-the-Loom fruits, "Hi, cuties. Whatcha doing in my laundry basket?" we smile as our curiosity is assuaged along with hers. Bill Cosby gets consumers tickled about the children in his Jell-O commercials, and strokes the need to nurture.

An insurance company wants to invoke the need to feel safe, but does not want to leave readers with an unpleasant aftertaste; cartoonist Rowland Wilson creates an avalanche about to crush a gentleman who is saying to another, "My insurance company? New England Life, of course. Why?" The same tactic of humor undercutting threat is used in the cartoon commercials for Safeco when the Pink Panther wanders from one disaster to another. Often humor masks aggression: comedian Bob Hope in the outfit of a boxer promises to knock out the knock-knocks with Texaco; Rodney Dangerfield, who "can't get no respect," invites aggression as the comic relief in Miller Lite commercials.

Roughly fifteen percent of all advertisements incorporate a celebrity, almost always from the fields of entertainment or sports. The approach can also prove troublesome for advertisers, for celebrities are human beings too, and fully capable of the most remarkable behavior. If anything distasteful about them emerges, it is likely to reflect on the product. The advertisers making use of Anita Bryant[20] and Billy Jean King[21] suffered several anxious moments. An untimely death can also react poorly on a product. But advertisers are willing to take risks because celebrities can be such a good link between producers and consumers, performing the social role of introducer.

There are several psychological needs these middlemen can play upon. Let's take the product class of cameras and see how different celebrities can hit different needs. The need for guidance can be invoked by Michael Landon, who plays such a wonderful dad on "Little House on the Prairie"; when he says to buy Kodak equipment, many people listen. James Garner for Polaroid cameras is put in a similar authoritative role, so defined by a mocking spouse. The need to achieve is summoned up by Tracy Austin and other tennis stars for Canon AE-1; the advertiser first makes sure we see these athletes playing to win. When Cheryl Tiegs[22] speaks up for Olympus cameras, it is the need for attention that is being targeted.

85 The past and future, being outside our grasp, are exploited by advertisers as locales for the projection of needs. History can offer up heroes (and call up the need to achieve) or traditions (need for guidance) as well as art objects (need for aesthetic sensations). Nostalgia is a kindly version of personal history and is deployed by advertisers to rouse needs for

affiliation and for guidance; the need to escape can come in here, too. The same need to escape is sometimes the point of futuristic appeals but picturing the avant-garde can also be a way to get at the need to achieve.

Analyzing Advertisements

When analyzing ads yourself for their emotional appeals, it takes a bit of practice to learn to ignore the product information (as well as one's own experience and feelings about the product). But that skill comes soon enough, as does the ability to quickly sort out from all the non-product aspects of an ad the chief element which is the most striking, the most likely to snag attention first and penetrate brains farthest. The key to the appeal, this element usually presents itself centrally and forwardly to the reader or viewer.

Another clue: the viewing angle which the audience has on the ad's subjects is informative. If the subjects are photographed or filmed from below and thus are looking down at you much as the Green Giant does, then the need to be guided is a good candidate for the ad's emotional appeal. If, on the other hand, the subjects are shot from above and appear deferential, as is often the case with children or female models, then other needs are being appealed to.

To figure out an ad's emotional appeal, it is wise to know (or have a good hunch about) who the targeted consumers are; this can often be inferred from the magazine or television show it appears in. This piece of information is a great help in determining the appeal and in deciding between two different interpretations. For example, if an ad features a partially undressed female, this would typically signal one appeal for readers of *Penthouse* (need for sex) and another for readers of *Cosmopolitan* (need for attention).

It would be convenient if every ad made just one appeal, were aimed at just one need. Unfortunately, things are often not that simple. A cigarette ad with a couple at the edge of a polo field is trying to hit both the need for affiliation and the need for prominence; depending on the attitude of the male, dominance could also be an ingredient in this. An ad for Chimere perfume incorporates two photos: in the top one the lady is being commanding at a business luncheon (need to dominate), but in the lower one she is being bussed (need for affiliation). Better ads, however, seem to avoid being too diffused; in the study of post-World War II advertising described earlier, appeals grew more focused as the decades passed. As a rule of thumb, about sixty percent have two conspicuous appeals; the last twenty percent have three or more. Rather than looking for the greatest number of appeals, decoding ads is most productive when the loudest one or two appeals are discerned, since those are the appeals with the best chance of grabbing people's attention.

90 Finally, analyzing ads does not have to be a solo activity and probably should not be. The greater number of people there are involved, the better chance there is of transcending individual biases and discerning the essential emotional lure built into an advertisement. 90

Do They or Don't They?

Do the emotional appeals made in advertisements add up to the sinister manipulation of consumers?

It is clear that these ads work. Attention is caught, communication occurs between producers and consumers, and sales result. It turns out to be difficult to detail the exact relationship between a specific ad and a specific purchase, or even between a campaign and subsequent sales figures, because advertising is only one of a host of influences upon consumption. Yet no one is fooled by this lack of perfect proof; everyone knows that advertising sells. If this were not the case, then tight-fisted American businesses would not spend a total of fifty billion dollars annually on these messages.

But before anyone despairs that advertisers have our number to the extent that they can marshal us at will and march us like automatons to the check-out counters, we should recall the resiliency and obduracy of the American consumer. Advertisers may have uncovered the softest spots in minds, but that does not mean they have found truly gaping apertures. There is no evidence that advertising can get people to do things contrary to their self-interests. Despite all the finesse of advertisements, and all the subtle emotional tugs, the public resists the vast majority of the petitions. According to the marketing division of the A. C. Nielsen Company, a whopping seventy-five percent of all new products die within a year in the marketplace, the victims of consumer disinterest which no amount of advertising could overcome. The appeals in advertising may be the most captivating there are to be had, but they are not enough to entrap the wily consumer.

The key to understanding the discrepancy between, on the one hand, the fact that advertising truly works, and, on the other, the fact that it hardly works, is to take into account the enormous numbers of people exposed to an ad. Modern-day communications permit an ad to be displayed to millions upon millions of individuals; if the smallest fraction of that audience can be moved to buy the product, then the ad has been successful. When one percent of the people exposed to a television advertising campaign reach for their wallets, that could be one million sales, which may be enough to keep the product in production and the advertisements coming.

95 In arriving at an evenhanded judgment about advertisements and their emotional appeals, it is good to keep in mind that many of the purchases which might be credited to these ads are experienced as genuinely gratifying to the consumer. We sincerely like the goods or service we have bought, and we may even like some of the emotional drapery that an ad suggests comes with it. It has sometimes been noted that the most avid students of advertisements are the people who have just bought the product; they want to steep themselves in the associated imagery. This may be the reason that Americans, when polled, are not negative about advertising and do not disclose any sense of being misused. The volume of advertising may be an irritant, but the product information as well as the imaginative material in ads are partial compensation. 95

A productive understanding is that advertising messages involve costs and benefits at both ends of the communications channel. For those few ads which do make contact, the consumer surrenders a moment of time, has the lower brain curried, and receives notice of a product; the advertiser has given up money and has increased the chance of sales. In this sort of communications activity, neither party can be said to be the loser.

End Notes

1. Brooke Shields was still a minor when she did the ads for Calvin Klein jeans. The ad was made more provocative with the tag line, "Nothing can get between me and my Calvins."
2. "Flick my Bic" was the slogan for a cigarette lighter.
3. Geritol was a product marketed to older people as a tonic for increasing energy.
4. Mickey Rooney was once a child actor and a versatile entertainer.
5. Quantas Airlines is an Australian airline that once used a koala bear in its marketing campaign.

6. Robert Young was a movie and television star. His most well-known television roles cast him as a confident and kind authority figure.
7. Florence Henderson was the mother on *The Brady Bunch.*
8. Orson Welles was a movie director and actor. Paul Masson wines used him as the spokesperson because of his cultural cache.
9. Brenda Vaccarro is a movie and television actress with a particularly smoky, sexy voice.
10. Mr. Goodwrench was the persona for an ad campaign intended to instill trust in auto mechanics.
11. E. F. Hutton was at one time one of the most respected brokerage firms in the U. S.
12. Don Rickles is a comedian known for using insult as a form of humor.
13. Lynda Carter played Wonder Woman on a television series.
14. O. J. Simpson at one time had a very appealing image as an athlete.
15. Reggie Jackson was one of the greatest home run hitters for the New York Yankees.
16. Cathy Rigby had twice been an Olympian and also World Champion in gymnastics. Her wholesome image took her to the Broadway stage.
17. Peggy Fleming had a great career as an elegant figure skater.
18. Shelly Hack was in the cast of the television show *Charlie's Angels.*
19. Karl Malden is a well-known actor who played a stern cop in the television show *The Streets of San Francisco.*
20. Anita Bryant, a former beauty queen, was known for her conservative, wholesome image.
21. Billy Jean King is one of the greatest tennis players of all time and was also a social activist.
22. Cheryl Tiegs was once a popular supermodel associated with *Sports Illustrated.*

Questions on Meaning

1. What is an appeal? Define it in your own words. What is the difference between an advertisement's appeal and its stylistic features? What does Fowles mean by "orders of content"?
2. Of the list of basic appeals, which ones seem most obvious to you based on your observations of ads? Do you agree with the apparent assumption that humans have a basic nature and are uniformly driven by all of these appeals on the level of the "lower brain"?
3. What is the purpose of a more acute understanding of how mass advertisements are geared to appeal to consumers? If, as Fowles suggests, people are not simply at the mercy of the advertisers, why do mass campaigns persist?

Questions on Rhetorical Strategy and Style

1. Why does Fowles make certain to acknowledge the work of Henry Murray? How does this enhance his credibility?
2. In what ways does this selection conform to the conventions of writing for the social sciences? In what ways does Fowles attempt to reach a more general audience? Has he been successful, in your opinion?
3. How would you characterize the last section of the essay? Why has the author reserved this discussion until after he has presented his analysis of the fifteen appeals?

Writing Assignments

1. Using Fowles's list of appeals, write an analysis of a group of five or six advertisements from a variety of magazines. Describe how easy or difficult it was for you to identify the appeals you recognized. Did you notice how different magazines ran ads emphasizing different appeals? What do these differences reflect about the character of each publication?
2. Most people agree that advertisers commonly use sex to sell their products. Yet, this emotional appeal can be deployed in variety of ways. Locate different examples of this use of an appeal. Write an essay in which you describe the similarities and differences in how this appeal is applied in these ads. What audiences are these ads directed toward?

Supplemental
Readings

The Story of an Hour

Kate Chopin

Kate Chopin (b. Katherine O'Flaherty, 1851–1904) began her life in St. Louis, Missouri. Her father died when she was four years old, so she was reared by three widows: her mother, her grandmother, and her great-grandmother. She was graduated from Sacred Heart convent in 1870 and then married Oscar Chopin, following him to New Orleans and later to his plantation in northern Louisiana. The mother of six children, she was widowed in 1882 and moved back to St. Louis where she began to write stories and publish in stylish literary magazines. Her novels, At Fault (1890) and The Awakening (1899), shocked conservative Victorian society but are praised by modern critics. Her collections of short stories, Bayou Folk (1894) and A Night in Acadie (1897) draw on her years of experience on a Louisiana plantation among Creole people. She died of a brain hemorrhage at only fifty-three. "The Story of an Hour" caused Chopin to be shunned by both her literary club and magazine publishers at the close of the nineteenth century, but it has persevered to become especially appealing to women in the late twentieth century.

1 Knowing that Mrs. Mallard was afflicted with a heart trouble, great care was taken to break to her as gently as possible the news of her husband's death.

It was her sister Josephine who told her, in broken sentences, veiled hints that revealed in half concealing. Her husband's friend Richards was there, too, near her. It was he who had been in the newspaper office when intelligence of the railroad disaster was received, with Brently Mallard's name leading the list of "killed." He had only taken the time to assure himself of its truth by a second telegram, and had hastened to forestall any less careful, less tender friend in bearing the sad message.

The Story of an Hour (1894)

She did not hear the story as many women have heard the same, with a paralyzed inability to accept its significance. She wept at once, with sudden, wild abandonment, in her sister's arms. When the storm of grief had spent itself she went away to her room alone. She would have no one follow her.

There stood, facing the open window, a comfortable, roomy armchair. Into this she sank, pressed down by a physical exhaustion that haunted her body and seemed to reach into her soul.

5 She could see in the open square before her house the tops of trees that were all aquiver with the new spring life. The delicious breath of rain was in the air. In the street below a peddler was crying his wares. The notes of a distant song which someone was singing reached her faintly, and countless sparrows were twittering in the eaves.

There were patches of blue sky showing here and there through the clouds that had met and piled above the other in the west facing her window.

She sat with her head thrown back upon the cushion of the chair, quite motionless, except when a sob came up into her throat and shook her, as a child who has cried itself to sleep continues to sob in its dreams.

She was young, with a fair, calm face, whose lines bespoke repression and even a certain strength. But now there was a dull stare in her eyes, whose gaze was fixed away off yonder on one of those patches of blue sky. It was not a glance of reflection, but rather indicated a suspension of intelligent thought.

There was something coming to her and she was waiting for it, fearfully. What was it? She did not know; it was too subtle and elusive to name. But she felt it, creeping out of the sky, reaching toward her through the sounds, the scents, the color that filled the air.

10 Now her bosom rose and fell tumultuously. She was beginning to recognize this thing that was approaching to possess her, and she was striving to beat it back with her will—as powerless as her two white slender hands would have been.

When she abandoned herself a little whispered word escaped her slightly parted lips. She said it over and over under her breath: "Free, free, free!" The vacant stare and the look of terror that had followed it went from her eyes. They stayed keen and bright. Her pulses beat fast, and the coursing blood warmed and relaxed every inch of her body.

She did not stop to ask if it were or were not a monstrous joy that held her. A clear and exalted perception enabled her to dismiss the suggestion as trivial.

She knew that she would weep again when she saw the kind, tender hands folded in death; the face that had never looked save with love upon her, fixed and gray and dead. But she saw beyond that bitter moment a long procession of years to come that would belong to her absolutely. And she opened and spread her arms out to them in welcome.

There would be no one to live for her during those coming years; she would live for herself. There would be no powerful will bending her in that blind persistence with which men and women believe they have a right to impose a private will upon a fellow-creature. A kind intention or a cruel intention made the act seem no less a crime as she looked upon it in that brief moment of illumination.

15 And yet she had loved him—sometimes. Often she had not. What 15 did it matter! What could love, the unsolved mystery, count for in face of this possession of self-assertion which she suddenly recognized as the strongest impulse of her being!

"Free! Body and soul free!" she kept whispering.

Josephine was kneeling before the closed door with her lips to the keyhole, imploring for admission. "Louise, open the door! I beg; open the door—you will make yourself ill. What are you doing, Louise? For heaven's sake open the door."

"Go away. I am not making myself ill." No; she was drinking in a very elixir of life through that open window.

Her fancy was running riot along those days ahead of her. Spring days, and summer days, and all sorts of days that would be her own. She breathed a quick prayer that life might be long. It was only yesterday she had thought with a shudder that life might be long.

20 She arose at length and opened the door to her sister's importu- 20 nities. There was a feverish triumph in her eyes, and she carried herself unwittingly like a goddess of Victory. She clasped her sister's waist, and together they descended the stairs. Richards stood waiting for them at the bottom.

Someone was opening the front door with a latchkey. It was Brently Mallard who entered, a little travel-stained, composedly carrying his grip-sack and umbrella. He had been far from the scene of accident, and did not even know there had been one. He stood amazed at Josephine's piercing cry; at Richards' quick motion to screen him from the view of his wife.

But Richards was too late.

When the doctors came they said she had died of heart disease— of joy that kills.

Salvation

Langston Hughes

Langston Hughes (1902–1967), a poet, short-story writer, essayist, and playwright, was born in Joplin, Missouri, and grew up in Kansas and Ohio. After graduating from high school (where he began writing poetry), Hughes spent 15 months in Mexico with his father, attended Columbia University for a year, worked as a seaman on cargo ships bound to Africa and Europe, and bused tables at a hotel in New York City. Later, he returned to school and graduated from Lincoln University (1929). Part of the "Harlem Renaissance" or "New Negro Renaissance"—and fiercely proud of his African-American heritage—Hughes often drew from Negro spirituals and blues and jazz in his literary work. Hughes was published in Amsterdam News, Crisis, The New Negro, *and many other periodicals. His books include the novel* Not Without Laughter *(1930); the short story collection* The Ways of White Folks *(1934); the play* The Mulatto *(1935); his autobiography* The Big Sea *(1940); and his poetry collections* The Weary Blues *(1926),* Shakespeare of Harlem *(1942),* Montage of a Dream Deferred *(1951), and* Ask Your Mama *(1961). This selection, which appeared first in* The Big Sea, *dramatizes an important event in Hughes's life.*

1   I was saved from sin when I was going on thirteen. But not really saved. It happened like this. There was a big revival at my Auntie Reed's church. Every night for weeks there had been much preaching, singing, praying, and shouting, and some very hardened sinners had been brought to Christ, and the membership of the church had

grown by leaps and bounds. Then just before the revival ended, they held a special meeting for children, "to bring the young lambs to the fold." My aunt spoke of it for days ahead. That night I was escorted to the front row and placed on the mourners' bench with all the other young sinners, who had not yet been brought to Jesus.

My aunt told me that when you were saved you saw a light, and something happened to you inside! And Jesus came into your life! And God was with you from then on! She said you could see and hear and feel Jesus in your soul. I believed her. I had heard a great many old people say that same thing and it seemed to me they ought to know. So I sat there calmly in the hot, crowded church, waiting for Jesus to come to me.

The preacher preached a wonderful rhythmical sermon, all moans and shouts and lonely cries and dire pictures of hell, and then he sang a song about the ninety and nine safe in the fold, but one little lamb was left out in the cold. Then he said: "Won't you come? Won't you come to Jesus? Young lambs, won't you come?" And he held out his arms to all us young sinners there on the mourners' bench. And the little girls cried. And some of them jumped up and went to Jesus right away. But most of us just sat there.

A great many old people came and knelt around us and prayed, old women with jet-black faces and braided hair, old men with work-gnarled hands. And the church sang a song about the lower lights are burning, some poor sinners to be saved. And the whole building rocked with prayer and song.

5   Still I kept waiting to *see* Jesus.   5

Finally all the young people had gone to the altar and were saved, but one boy and me. He was a rounder's son named Westley. Westley and I were surrounded by sisters and deacons praying. It was very hot in the church, and getting late now. Finally Westley said to me in a whisper: "God damn! I'm tired o' sitting here. Let's get up and be saved." So he got up and was saved.

Then I was left all alone on the mourners' bench. My aunt came and knelt at my knees and cried, while prayers and song swirled all around me in the little church. The whole congregation prayed for me alone in a mighty wail of moans and voices. And I kept waiting serenely for Jesus, waiting, waiting—but he didn't come. I wanted to see him, but nothing happened to me. Nothing! I wanted something to happen to me, but nothing happened.

I heard the songs and the minister saying: "Why don't you come? My dear child, why don't you come to Jesus? Jesus is waiting for you. He wants you. Why don't you come? Sister Reed, what is this child's name?"

"Langston," my aunt sobbed.

10 "Langston, why don't you come? Why don't you come and be 10 saved? Oh, Lamb of God! Why don't you come?"

Now it was really getting late. I began to be ashamed of myself, holding everything up so long. I began to wonder what God thought about Westley, who certainly hadn't seen Jesus either, but who was now sitting proudly on the platform, swinging his knickerbockered legs and grinning down at me, surrounded by deacons and old women on their knees praying. God had not struck Westley dead for taking his name in vain or for lying in the temple. So I decided that maybe to save further trouble, I'd better lie, too, and say that Jesus had come, and get up and be saved.

So I got up.

Suddenly the whole room broke into a sea of shouting, as they saw me rise. Waves of rejoicing swept the place. Women leaped in the air. My aunt threw her arms around me. The minister took me by the hand and led me to the platform.

When things quieted down, in a hushed silence, punctuated by a few ecstatic "Amens," all the new young lambs were blessed in the name of God. Then joyous singing filled the room.

15 That night, for the last time in my life but one—for I was a big 15 boy twelve years old—I cried. I cried, in bed alone, and couldn't stop. I buried my head under the quilts, but my aunt heard me. She woke up and told my uncle I was crying because the Holy Ghost had come into my life, and because I had seen Jesus. But I was really crying because I couldn't bear to tell her that I had lied, that I had deceived everybody in the church, that I hadn't seen Jesus, and that now I didn't believe there was a Jesus any more, since he didn't come to help me.

The Myth of Sisyphus

Albert Camus

*Albert Camus (1913–1960) was born in Mondovi, Alge-
ria (at that time a colony of France). Camus attended the
University of Algeria, where he majored in philosophy. He
wrote for the* Alger-Republican, *a socialist paper, between
1937 and 1939, and edited* Soir-Republican, *another socialist paper, from 1939–1940. He moved to France during World War II, joined the Resistance, and wrote for and
edited the underground publication* Combat. *A leading
proponent of existentialism, Camus is perhaps best remembered for* The Rebel: An Essay on Man in Revolt *(1954),
for which he received the Nobel Prize for Literature
(1957). Other books by Camus include* The Myth of Sisyphus *(1942), his first collection of philosophical essays, and
the novels* The Stranger *(1942),* The Plague *(1947),* The
Fall *(1956), and* Exile and the Kingdom *(1957). In this
story, Camus analyzes the meaning and impact of the fate
of Sisyphus—a symbol of the human condition.*

1   The gods had condemned Sisyphus to ceaselessly rolling a rock
to the top of a mountain, whence the stone would fall back of
its own weight. They had thought with some reason that there
is no more dreadful punishment than futile and hopeless labor.

If one believes Homer, Sisyphus was the wisest and most prudent
of mortals. According to another tradition, however, he was disposed
to practice the profession of highwayman. I see no contradiction in
this. Opinions differ as to the reasons why he became the futile laborer
of the underworld. To begin with, he is accused of a certain levity in
regard to the gods. He stole their secrets. Aegina, the daughter of

Aesopus, was carried off by Jupiter. The father was shocked by that disappearance and complained to Sisyphus. He, who knew of the abduction, offered to tell about it on condition that Aesopus would give water to the citadel of Corinth. To the celestial thunderbolts he preferred the benediction of water. He was punished for this in the underworld. Homer tells us also that Sisyphus had put Death in chains. Pluto could not endure the sight of his deserted, silent empire. He dispatched the god of war, who liberated Death from the hands of her conqueror.

It is said also that Sisyphus, being near to death, rashly wanted to test his wife's love. He ordered her to cast his unburied body into the middle of the public square. Sisyphus woke up in the underworld. And there, annoyed by an obedience so contrary to human love, he obtained from Pluto permission to return to earth in order to chastise his wife. But when he had seen again the face of this world, enjoyed water and sun, warm stones and the sea, he no longer wanted to go back to the infernal darkness. Recalls, signs of anger, warnings were of no avail. Many years more he lived facing the curve of the gulf, the sparkling sea, and the smiles of earth. A decree of the gods was necessary. Mercury came and seized the impudent man by the collar and, snatching him from his joys, led him forcibly back to the underworld, where his rock was ready for him.

You have already grasped that Sisyphus is the absurd hero. He *is*, as much through his passions as through his torture. His scorn of the gods, his hatred of death, and his passion for life won him that unspeakable penalty in which the whole being is exerted toward accomplishing nothing. This is the price that must be paid for the passions of this earth. Nothing is told us about Sisyphus in the underworld. Myths are made for the imagination to breathe life into them. As for this myth, one sees merely the whole effort of a body straining to raise the huge stone, to roll it and push it up a slope a hundred times over; one sees the face screwed up, the cheek tight against the stone, the shoulder bracing the clay-covered mass, the foot wedging it, the fresh start with arms outstretched, the wholly human security of two earth-clotted hands. At the very end of his long effort measured by skyless space and time without depth, the purpose is achieved. Then Sisyphus watches the stone rush down in a few moments toward that lower world whence he will have to push it up again toward the summit. He goes back down to the plain.

5   It is during that return, that pause, that Sisyphus interests me. A   5
face that toils so close to stones is already stone itself! I see that man
going back down with a heavy yet measured step toward the torment
of which he will never know the end. That hour like a breathing-space
which returns as surely as his suffering, that is the hour of consciousness. At each of those moments when he leaves the heights and gradually sinks toward the lairs of the gods, he is superior to his fate. He
is stronger than his rock.

If this myth is tragic, that is because its hero is conscious. Where
would his torture be, indeed, if at every step the hope of succeeding
upheld him? The workman of today works every day in his life at the
same tasks, and his fate is no less absurd. But it is tragic only at the
rare moments when it becomes conscious. Sisyphus, proletarian of the
gods, powerless and rebellious, knows the whole extent of his
wretched condition: it is what he thinks of during his descent. The lu-
cidity that was to constitute his torture at the same time crowns his
victory. There is no fate that cannot be surmounted by scorn.

If the descent is thus sometimes performed in sorrow, it can also
take place in joy. This word is not too much. Again I fancy Sisyphus
returning toward his rock, and the sorrow was in the beginning. When
the images of earth cling too tightly to memory, when the call of happiness becomes too insistent, it happens that melancholy rises in man's
heart: this is the rock's victory, this is the rock itself. The boundless
grief is too heavy to bear. These are our nights of Gethsemane. But
crushing truths perish from being acknowledged. Thus, Oedipus at
the outset obeys fate without knowing it. But from the moment he
knows, his tragedy begins. Yet at the same moment, blind and desperate, he realizes that the only bond linking him to the world is the
cool hand of a girl. Then a tremendous remark rings out: "Despite so
many ordeals, my advanced age and the nobility of my soul make me
conclude that all is well." Sophocles' Oedipus, like Dostoevsky's Kir-
ilov, thus gives the recipe for the absurd victory. Ancient wisdom con-
firms modern heroism.

One does not discover the absurd without being tempted to write
a manual of happiness. "What! by such narrow ways—?" There is but
one world, however. Happiness and the absurd are two sons of the
same earth. They are inseparable. It would be a mistake to say that

happiness necessarily springs from the absurd discovery. It happens as well that the feeling of the absurd springs from happiness. "I conclude that all is well," says Oedipus, and that remark is sacred. It echoes in the wild and limited universe of man. It teaches that all is not, has not been, exhausted. It drives out of this world a god who had come into it with dissatisfaction and a preference for futile sufferings. It makes of fate a human matter, which must be settled among men.

All Sisyphus' silent joy is contained therein. His fate belongs to him. His rock is his thing. Likewise, the absurd man, when he contemplates his torment, silences all the idols. In the universe suddenly restored to its silence, the myriad wondering little voices of the earth rise up. Unconscious, secret calls, invitations from all the faces, they are the necessary reverse and price of victory. There is no sun without shadow, and it is essential to know the night. The absurd man says yes and his effort will henceforth be unceasing. If there is a personal fate, there is no higher destiny, or at least there is but one which he concludes is inevitable and despicable. For the rest, he knows himself to be the master of his days. At that subtle moment when man glances backward over his life, Sisyphus returning toward his rock, in that slight pivoting he contemplates that series of unrelated actions which becomes his fate, created by him, combined under his memory's eye and soon sealed by his death. Thus, convinced of the wholly human origin of all that is human, a blind man eager to see who knows that the night has no end, he is still on the go. The rock is still rolling.

10   I leave Sisyphus at the foot of the mountain! One always finds   10 one's burden again. But Sisyphus teaches the higher fidelity that negates the gods and raises rocks. He too concludes that all is well. This universe henceforth without a master seems to him neither sterile nor futile. Each atom of that stone, each mineral flake of that night-filled mountain, in itself forms a world. The struggle itself toward the heights is enough to fill a man's heart. One must imagine Sisyphus happy.

The Allegory of the Cave

Plato

Plato (c. 428–347 B.C.), one of the most influential philosophers in history, was born into a wealthy, aristocratic family, presumably in Athens. A pupil of Socrates (and teacher of Aristotle), Plato left Athens for nearly 20 years after his mentor's death in 399 B.C. Upon his return in 380 B.C., he established the Academy and taught there for the remainder of his life. Much of Plato's philosophy appears in his "dialogues"—conversations between Socrates and his students. Three of these "dialogues," the Apology, *the* Crito, *and the* Phaedo, *immortalized Socrates' trial and final days. Other well-known works of Plato include the* Republic *and* Laws. *Plato's belief in the separate existence of the body and soul and the existence of an eternal order of Forms (the Theory of Forms) have influenced Western thought for more than 2,000 years. In "The Allegory of the Cave" (from the* Republic), *Plato argues the need to differentiate between the world of the senses and physical phenomena and the world of knowledge.*

1   *Socrates:* And now, I said, let me show in a figure how far our nature is enlightened or unenlightened:— Behold! human beings living in an underground den, which has a mouth open towards the light and reaching all along the den; here they have been from their childhood, and have their legs and necks chained so that they cannot move, and can only see before them, being prevented by the chains from turning round their heads. Above and behind them a fire is blazing at a distance, and between the fire and the prisoners there is a raised way; and you will

The den, the prisoners: the light at a distance;   1

see, if you look, a low wall built along the way, like the screen which marionette players have in front of them, over which they show the puppets.

Glaucon: I see.

And do you see, I said, men passing along the wall carrying all sorts of vessels, and statues and figures of animals made of wood and stone and various materials, which appear over the wall? Some of them are talking, others silent.

You have shown me a strange image, and they are strange prisoners.

5   Like ourselves, I replied; and they see only their own shadows, or the shadows of one another, which the fire throws on the opposite wall of the cave?

The low wall, and the moving figures of which the shadows are seen on the opposite wall of the den. 5

True, he said; how could they see anything but the shadows if they were never allowed to move their heads?

And of the objects which are being carried in like manner they would only see the shadows?

Yes, he said.

And if they were able to converse with one another, would they not suppose that they were naming what was actually before them?

10   Very true.   10

And suppose further that the prison had an echo which came from the other side, would they not be sure to fancy when one of the passersby spoke that the voice which they heard came from the passing shadow?

The prisoners would mistake the shadows for realities.

No question, he replied.

To them, I said, the truth would be literally nothing but the shadows of the images.

That is certain.

15   And now look again, and see what will naturally follow if the prisoners are released and disabused of their error. At first, when any of them is liberated and compelled suddenly to stand up and turn his neck round and walk and look towards the light, he will suffer sharp pains; the glare will distress him, and he will be unable to see the realities of which in his former

And when released, they would still persist in maintaining the superior truth of the shadows. 15

state he had seen the shadows; and then conceive some one saying to him, that what he saw before was an illusion, but that now, when he is approaching nearer to being and his eye is turned towards more real existence, he has a clearer vision—what will be his reply? And you may further imagine that his instructor is pointing to the objects as they pass and requiring him to name them—will he not be perplexed? Will he not fancy that the shadows which he formerly saw are truer than the objects which are now shown to him?

Far truer.

And if he is compelled to look straight at the light, will he not have a pain in his eyes which will make him turn away to take refuge in the objects of vision which he can see, and which he will conceive to be in reality clearer than the things which are now being shown to him?

True, he said.

And suppose once more, that he is reluctantly dragged up a steep and rugged ascent, and held fast until he is forced into the presence of the sun himself, is he not likely to be pained and irritated? When he approaches the light his eyes will be dazzled, and he will not be able to see anything at all of what are now called realities.

When dragged upwards, they would be dazzled by excess of light.

20   Not all in a moment, he said.   20

He will require to grow accustomed to the sight of the upper world. And first he will see the shadows best, next the reflections of men and other objects in the water, and then the objects themselves; then he will gaze upon the light of the moon and the stars and the spangled heaven; and he will see the sky and the stars by night better than the sun or the light of the sun by day?

Certainly.

Last of all he will be able to see the sun, and not mere reflections of him in the water, but he will see him in his own proper place, and not in another; and he will contemplate him as he is.

At length they will see the sun and understand his nature.

Certainly.

25   He will then proceed to argue that this is he who gives the season and the years, and is the guardian of all that is in the visible world, and in a certain way the cause of all things which he and his fellows have been accustomed to behold?

Clearly, he said, he would first see the sun and then reason about him.

And when he remembered his old habitation, and the wisdom of the den and his fellow-prisoners, do you not suppose that he would felicitate himself on the change, and pity them?

They would then pity their old companions of the den.

Certainly, he would.

And if they were in the habit of conferring honours among themselves on those who were quickest to observe the passing shadows and to remark which of them went before, and which followed after, and which were together; and who were therefore best able to draw conclusions as to the future, do you think that he would care for such honors and glories, or envy the possessors of them? Would he not say with Homer, "Better to be the poor servant of a poor master," and to endure anything, rather than think as they do and live after their manner?

30   Yes, he said, I think that he would rather suffer anything than entertain those false notions and live in this miserable manner.

Imagine once more, I said, such as one coming suddenly out of the sun to be replaced in his old situation; would he not be certain to have his eyes full of darkness?

To be sure, he said.

And if there were a contest, and he had to compete in measuring the shadows with the prisoners who had never moved out of the den, while his sight was still weak, and before his eyes had become steady (and the time which would be needed to acquire this new habit of sight might be very considerable) would he not be ridiculous? Men would say of him that up

But when they returned to the den they would see much worse than those who had never left it.

he went and down he came without his eyes; and that it was better not even to think of ascending; and if any one tried to loose another and lead him up to the light, let them only catch the offender, and they would put him to death.

No question, he said.

35   This entire allegory, I said, you may now append, dear Glaucon, to the previous argument; the prison-house is the world of sight, the light of the fire is the sun, and you will not misapprehend me if you interpret the journey upwards to be the ascent of the soul into the intellectual world according to my poor belief, which, at your desire, I have expressed—whether rightly or wrongly God knows. But, whether true or false, my opinion is that in the world of knowledge the idea of good appears last of all, and is seen only with an effort; and when seen, is also inferred to be the universal author of all things beautiful and right, parent of light and of the lord of light in this visible world, and the immediate source of reason and truth in the intellectual; and that this is the power upon which he who would act rationally either in public or private life must have his eye fixed.

I agree, he said, as far as I am able to understand you.

The prison is the world of sight, the light of the fire is the sun.   35

Documentation in the Humanities: MLA Style

D ocumentation is like traffic signs and signals: Everyone in a culture agrees to use them in a certain way so that nobody gets hurt. Communities of readers and writers do the same thing: They agree to identify their sources according to a given set of rules. There are several forms of documentation for particular areas of study and specific journals.

The Modern Language Association of America is an international organization of teachers and researchers dedicated to the study and teaching of language and literature. Many humanities departments in schools and colleges as well as a host of journals and magazines require that writers use the MLA style when presenting a manuscript. The details of MLA style are presented in two books, the *MLA Handbook for Writers of Research Papers*, used mostly by high school and undergraduate college students; and the *MLA Style Manual and Guide to Scholarly Publishing*, used by graduate students, scholars, and professional writers).

MLA Manuscript Format

In addition to the many, many specifics of preparing a manuscript in MLA style, the following general rules apply.

Page layout:

- Use standard 8-1/2 by 11 paper and standard typeface. Avoid odd typefaces or other unusual variations available with word processing.
- Place name, date, and course information in the upper left-hand corner of the first page; double-space before the centered title.
- Double-space between lines.
- Leave at least one inch margins.

- Place page numbers in the upper right-hand corner, one half inch from the top of the paper; include your last name before the number for identification.

In the body of the paper:

- Cite sources in the text, not in footnotes or endnotes.
- Don't use punctuation between the author's name and the page number in a citation.
- Cite the page number(s) of direct quotations in in-text citations.
- Indent the first line of each paragraph five spaces.
- Indent quotations more than four typed lines ten spaces; omit the quotation marks.
- Leave one space after all punctuation; MLA allows either a single or a double space after periods or question and exclamation marks.
- Form a dash with two hyphens, using no spaces.

In the list of sources:

- Center the words "Works Cited" on the top of the page.
- List sources alphabetically by author's last name. If there is no author, alphabetize by book or selection title.
- Use hanging indentation (first line flush left against the margin, second and subsequent lines indented).
- Separate items in a citation (author, title, place and date of publication) with periods.
- If the city of publication is not easily recognizable, add a two-letter abbreviation for the state.

IN-TEXT CITATION

1. Author named in text
If the author is named in the text, only page numbers are given.

> Stephen Jay Gould discusses the power of
> scientific drawings (18).

2. Author not named in text
When the author is not named in the text, the name appears in the notation.

> Deep time appears as a new concept in
> Lavoisier (Gould 22).

3. Two or three authors
Use only the last names of the authors.

> Scharton and Neuleib claim that professors
> change when they work with writing centers
> (65).

4. Four or more authors
All four authors may be named, or author number one and "et al." (Latin for "et alia" which means "and others") may be referenced in the text or in parentheses.

> Duin, Lammers, Mason, and Graves suggest that
> mentors with much teaching experience will
> give more help than mentors who have taught
> little (143).

> Mentors with much teaching experience will
> give more help than mentors who have taught
> little (Duin et al. 143).

5. Unknown author
The title substitutes for the author's name in the text or in parentheses.

> "The Twin Corbies" refers to crows (119).

6. Corporate author

A corporate author can be named in either the text or in the parentheses.

```
Illinois State University notes that it
employs 264 professors (1).
```

7. Two or more works by the same author

When two or more works by one author appear on the Works Cited page, either name the work in the text, or include a short form of the title in the parentheses.

```
In "The Gift of Insight," Neuleib and
Scharton explain the complexities of type
preference (197).
```

If author and shortened form both appear in parentheses, use this form:

```
(Neuleib and Scharton, "Insight" 197).
```

8. A source quoted in another source

To show that one author is quoting another, use the abbreviation "qtd. in."

```
Flower notes that "research in composition
shows an alternative picture of how knowledge
can be developed" (qtd. in Neuleib and
Scharton 54).
```

9. Novel, play, or poem

Give the title if not mentioned in text when the work is first referred to, then follow with specific information as listed below.

Novel: part or chapter
```
Ged said, "I fear what follows behind me"
(A Wizard of Earthsea 117: ch. 6).
```

Play: act and scene and line numbers in Arabic numerals
```
"He waxes desperate with imagination," cries
Horatio (Hamlet 1.4.87).
```

Poem: refer to the part (if applicable) and line numbers

```
"Surely some revelation is at hand," muses
Yeats's "The Second Coming" (10).
```

10. Work in an anthology

Cite the author's name, not the editor's name.

```
In his essay "On Stories," Lewis observes
that "No book is really worth reading at the
age of ten which is not equally worth reading
at the age of fifty" (100).
```

11. Entire work

Name the author in the text or note in parentheses.

```
Freire was introduced to North American
scholars in Freire for the Classroom (Shor).
```

WORKS CITED

Books

1. One author

```
LeGuin, Ursula K. A Wizard of Earthsea. New
    York: Ace, 1968.
```

2. Two or three authors

```
Scharton, Maurice, and Janice Neuleib. Inside/
    Out: A Guide to Writing. Needham Heights,
    MA: Allyn & Bacon, 1992.
```

3. More than three authors or editors

```
Lawson, Bruce, et al., eds. Encountering Stu-
    dent Texts. Urbana: NCTE, 1989.
```

4. Editor

```
Hooper, Walter, ed. The Letters of C. S. Lewis.
    New York: Macmillan, 1979.
```

5. Author with editor

```
Tolkien, J.R.R. The Tolkien Reader. Ed.
    Christopher Tolkien. New York: Ballantine,
    1966.
```

6. Unknown author

```
Primary Colors. New York: Random House, 1996.
```

7. Corporate author

```
Illinois State University. Facts 1998-9. Nor-
    mal, IL: Illinois State UP, 1999.
```

8. Two or more works by the same author

```
Lewis, C. S. The Lion, the Witch, and the
    Wardrobe. New York: Macmillan, 1950.

---. The Magician's Nephew. New York: Macmil-
    lan, 1955.
```

9. Translation

```
Tolstoy, L. N. Anna Karenina. Trans. Rosemary
    Edmunds. New York: Viking, 1954.
```

10. Work in an anthology

```
Walsh, Chad. "The Reeducation of the Fearful
    Pilgrim." The Longing for a Form. Ed.
    Peter J. Schakel. Kent, OH: Kent State UP,
    1977. 64-72.
```

Periodicals

11. Newspaper article
(signed)

```
Flick, Bill. "This Year in History." Daily
    Pantagraph 31 Dec. 1998: A14.
```

(unsigned)

"Honda Motor Recalls Several Models to Fix
Ball-Joint Assembly." <u>Wall Street Journal</u>
13 May 1999: B14.

12. Magazine article

(signed)

Gould, Stephen Jay. "Capturing the Center."
<u>Natural History</u> Dec. 1998: 14+.

(unsigned)

"College Can Give You Grief." <u>Psychology
Today</u> Oct. 1998: 20.

13. Journal article

(with continuous page numbering from issue to issue within a year)

Fleckenstein, Kristie. "Writing Bodies." <u>Col-
lege English</u> 61 (1999): 281-306.

(with each issue paged separately)

Becker, Becky K. "Women Who Choose: The Theme
of Mothering in Selected Dramas." <u>American
Drama</u> 6.2 (1997): 43+.

[note that "6.2" means vol. 6, issue #2]

Other Sources

14. The Bible

<u>The New International Bible</u>. Colorado
Springs: International Bible Society,
1972.

[The King James Bible need not be named or underlined. You need only note chapter and verse in parentheses in the text (Matt:12.1-3). Translations of the Bible other than King James should be identified and underlined.]

15. Letter to the editor

> White, Curt. Letter. <u>The Vidette</u>. 18 Feb.
>   1999: 6.

16. Personal or telephone interview

> Kay, Martha. Personal interview. 10 Mar.
>   1999.

17. Record, tape, or CD

> Kingston Trio. <u>Greatest Hits</u>. Curb Records,
>   1991.

Electronic Sources

These sources include a variety of types of communication: personal e-mail between persons or among private group members, listservs among several individuals with common work or interests, or news groups that serve associations or subscribers. The World Wide Web connects the individual to a wider community, including businesses and other commercial groups. For all these sources, documentation should be used consistently. Note that the second date is always the date a website was accessed while the first date is the time of publication.

18. Professional site

> <u>NCTE Home Page</u>. 6 January 2004. National Coun-
>   cil of Teachers of English. 4 Mar. 2004
>   <http://www.ncte.org>.

19. A personal site

> Neuleib, Janice Witherspoon. Home page. Illi-
>   nois State University. 26 Feb. 2004 <http://
>   www.ilstu.edu/~jneuleib>.

20. A book

> Crane, Stephen. <u>The Red Badge of Courage</u>. Gut-
>   tenberg Project. <u>University of California
>   Berkeley Archives</u>. 4 Sept. 1996. Sunsite

Berkeley. 4 Mar. 2004 <http://sunsite.
berkeley.edu/Literature/Crane/RedBadge/>.

21. A poem
Dickinson, Emily. "A Narrow Fellow in the
Grass," <u>Poetry Archive</u>.
<http://www.emule.com/poetry<.

22. An article in a reference database
"On 'Behave.'" <u>Oxford English Dictionary On-
line</u>. Second Edition. 1989. Oxford English
Dictionary. 5 Mar. 2004
<http://dictionary.oed.com/cgi/entry/00019662>.

23. An article in a journal
Applebee, Arthur N., and Judith A. Langer.
"Discussion-Based Approaches to Student Understanding: Classroom Instruction in the
Middle School Classroom." <u>American Education Research Journal</u> 40:3 (2003). 2 Mar.
2004. <http://www.ncte.org/about/research/
articles/115102.htm>.

24. An article in a magazine
Perkins, Sid. "Avalanche." <u>Science News On Line</u>
2 Mar. 2002. 16 Feb. 2004 <http://www. sci-
encenews.org/articles/20020302/bob14.asp>.

25. A review
Traister, Rebecca. "Is 'The Sopranos' a Chick
Flick?" Rev. of <u>The Sopranos TV Series</u>.<u>Salon</u>
6 Mar. 2004. 8 Mar. 2004. <www.salon.com
.mwt/feature/2004/03/06/carmela_soprano/
index_mp.html>

26. A posting to a discussion group

Hesse, Doug. "What Makes a College Good." Online
    posting. 5 Nov. 2003. ISU Teach. 7 Mar. 2004
    <isuteach@listserv.ilstu.edu>.

27. A personal e-mail message

Neuleib, Janice. "Collaborative MR Chapter."
    E-mail to Katherine Gretz. 19 Feb. 2004.